First Habits Win

Prime your children for a lifetime of financial success with this simple system.

Bonus:

Take the Money Mindset and Money Personality quizzes to determine how you are influencing your children's attitudes about money.

By Mike Miller

Cover design by Justin Oswald

Edited by Amy Bauer

Interior pagination by Entsbough Publishing Services LLC

www.firsthabitswin.com

First Habits Win/Mike Miller – 1st ed.

ISBN: 9798514702398

I'm dedicating this book to my wife, Denise,
our three beautiful daughters, Lauren, Hayley and Anna,
and my parents, who have been such positive role models
for our whole family.

Lauren, Hayley and Anna,
we are so proud of the young ladies you have become!

Table of Contents

Author's Note

As I complete this book, it is May 2021. We've just come through more than a year of pandemic precautions, and the light at the end of the tunnel seems to be growing brighter. But we have some scars.

The COVID-19 virus led to the unemployment of tens of millions of Americans, and the unemployment rate remains nearly double pre-pandemic levels. Trillions of stimulus dollars have been poured into the economy to avoid the next Great Depression. After a contentious national election, political discord remains at an all time high, and racial tensions have divided our nation.

As millions of people around the world have been on heightened alert about their physical health and safety during the pandemic, financial health also remains top of mind.

How much of my retirement savings was lost? What if I lose my job? What if my kids lose their jobs and move back home? How long can I provide for my family with my current savings? Could I lose my car, my house, my business?

Money is a constant in our lives, and we must be prepared to manage it well in any circumstance. That's why I wrote "First Habits Win" and developed the First Habits system. I want to empower parents, just like you, to help your children thrive and feel confident about their financial outlook no matter what the future holds.

Summary

I hate having to read through the justification and supporting evidence for an idea before hearing what it is, so I will begin this book with the summary.

When each of our daughters turned 12 years old, I gave them control of managing their own bank accounts and planning their own expenses. More specifically, I went through the prior year's expenses and calculated what we had spent on clothes, school, sports and other extracurricular activities, entertainment, and gifts. I added some money to account for expenses I'm sure I overlooked, and then I divided that total by 12. This was the monthly allowance we provided. I set up a spreadsheet to track planned monthly expenses and large future expenses that would need to be saved for over time. This would become the earning, spending, saving and gifting plan they would use to create a systematic way to manage their money.

This is the basis of the First Habits system detailed in this book. With the benefit of hindsight, I have shared what I would change and what I would add to this system to further improve the educational experience. The major additions — since using the system with our daughters — include defining your child's Money Personality and your own Money Mindset. These two critical factors have an enormous influence on how we all manage our financial lives, including everything from limiting the accumulation of wealth and income to defining our self-worth by our net worth. The smaller, but equally critical, changes I have added include an additional focus on savings. Specifically, paying yourself first before considering the expenses you can afford and adding additional responsibility as children progress in the system.

Our daughters are now all in their twenties and financially independent. This system allowed them to make mistakes and learn lessons from those mistakes early in life while much less was at stake. The system helped them build habits for managing their money and taught them valuable lessons that equipped them to be financially responsible and independent.

The First Habits system creates good money management habits by combining parental instruction and oversight with hands-on experience earning, saving, spending and giving during a child's middle and high school years. The system also guides parents on how to positively influence their child's Money Mindset to help them build a healthy relationship with money.

To help you get started and manage the First Habits system with your children, I've developed a free app and a downloadable spreadsheet. The Cabbage app is available for Apple users on the App Store and for Android users at Google Play. The free downloadable Excel planning spreadsheet is available on the First Habits Win website, www.FirstHabitsWin.com. At the site, you'll also find Money Personality and Money Mindset quizzes and other useful resources.

While I applaud schools across the country for adding personal finance courses to their curriculum, I don't believe the lessons will stick without the hands-on experience. How much do you remember from the high school subjects you don't use every day? Math, Science, English ... It is not enough to learn a skill; you need to practice and develop the skill to get the benefits. That's why the First Habits system is meant to be taught by parents during a child's formative years.

Three Keys to Success

- Discipline
- Patience
- Persistence

Remembering core lessons from the First Habits system: the **MONEY** acronym.

Make sure to pay yourself first.

Only use a credit card if you pay the total balance each month.

Never compare yourself to others.

Everyone makes mistakes; learn from them.

Your most important decision is the next one.

THIS DOESN'T COST YOU A NICKEL!

As I have explained this system to parents, I've heard a common misunderstanding that I want to clear up. Some parents have told me, "That sounds great Mike, but I just can't afford it." Let me be clear. **There is no additional cost to implement this system with your children**. In fact, you will likely *save money*.

We are simply taking the money you would already spend on your children and giving them control of it. Right now, you pay for their clothes and school supplies and sports. With the First Habits system, you give the money to them and they pay for these things.

Why could this lead to savings? Because your children will probably be more frugal with their spending once they are in charge of it.

Introduction

Let's face it, many of us have a lot of anxiety when it comes to money. Over the years, I've talked to many successful adults who freely admit the problems they've had with credit cards, uncontrolled spending, taxes and countless other money issues.

I've watched their financial struggles manifest into short- and long-term side effects that include physical illness, depression and the breaking up of relationships, marriages and families.

The First Habits System

After introducing a simple planning and tracking program to our three daughters, starting when each turned 12, I witnessed them become confident and self-assured at managing their own money. While our daughters can't understand what it would be like to not have this training and experience, they have each acknowledged witnessing their friends and classmates struggle with simple money issues that they have been able to avoid because of the First Habits system.

The key difference between this system and other financial education programs is hands-on practical experience. While academic components are key to teaching, it's the experience that cements the learning and leads to habit formation and ultimately confidence.

I have developed this system — First Habits — into something easy for parents to implement and manage in the hope of carving out a new path for *future generations* by starting early training on personal financial management taught by their most trusted teacher: you! The system outlined in this book is not exactly what I implemented with our daughters — it has grown and expanded from the lessons we learned. The system our daughters completed included planning and paying for the expenses I assigned to them. While I noticed differences in each of our daughters and worked with each uniquely to better meet their needs, at the time I did not initially identify them as having unique money personalities. I have added a section on Money Personality, and I've also created a Money Personality quiz. You will start by identifying your own Money Personality. With that understanding, you will then be able to identify your child's Money Personality based on their behavior as they start this system. This will help you tailor the system to meet their unique needs.

I was also unaware of the Money Mindset and how *my* experiences and attitude toward money would influence our children. As I have learned more about behavioral finance and the impact that we have on forming our children's attitudes toward earning, spending, saving, being charitable and accumulating wealth, I believe this section is the most impactful addition to the program. I have added a Money Mindset quiz to determine your personal Money Mindset and make you aware of how your actions and your mindset influences your child.

Identifying your child's specific Money Personality and planning your influence with an understanding of the Money Mindset will yield substantially greater benefits.

Throughout the book, I've included "If I Had It To Do Over" sections with tips that became clear to me in hindsight as our daughters completed the system. These are situational but should provide you with some insightful guidance as you navigate the system with your child.

The First Habits system has provided great results for my family, and I hope it will help yours, too.

The Benefits

Think about it: Your greatest legacy could be helping your children feel *confident* about earning, spending and saving money from an early age, while also influencing their Money Mindset toward a positive and healthy attitude around money and wealth.

As you guide your children through the First Habits system, expect the following benefits:

- Their confidence will grow, and they will be more self-assured.
- They will develop a healthy and positive Money Mindset.
- Over time, their fears about money and the stigma associated with money will disappear.
- You will save yourself thousands or tens of thousands of dollars versus just giving money to your children as needed. (Hint: Put it toward their college fund. We saved tens of thousands.)
- Ultimately, you will spare your children the potential anxiety and problems caused by being *uneducated* about money.

What if you haven't done a good job of managing your *own* money? Don't worry. You can still teach your children good habits, and you might even pick up some tips from the First Habits system that can help you as well. The one thing I would strongly warn against is sharing your financial problems with your children. You can and should discuss family financial matters openly, but don't weigh your children down with your financial burdens.

For example, as you sit down to pay bills, invite your child to join you and talk through what you're doing. Keep it simple, straightforward and upbeat. For example:

> *"I always pay our bills on payday, when I get my*
> *paycheck from work. I do this because I want to make*
> *sure to take care of the bills that must be paid first. If I*

went out to buy clothes or even groceries before paying the bills, I might spend too much and not have enough left to pay for the house payment or the electric bill."

Rather than:

"Paying bills is the worst part of my week. We put a bunch of stuff on the credit card to pay for Christmas, and now we barely have enough for groceries after we pay the credit card bill on top of everything else."

The first example shows your child that paying bills is a task that needs to be done, while explaining the reasons why and how you do it as a responsible adult. The second example teaches your child that paying bills is a huge negative to be dreaded — and that Christmas is causing a financial burden. Both conversations are influencing your child's Money Mindset, but one is positive and the other negative.

SECTION ONE

Raising *Confident,* Successful Adults

The best way to build confidence in a given area is to invest energy in it and work hard at it.

– Tony Schwartz, author of "Be Excellent at Anything"

A PARENT'S JOB

As parents, we know it is our responsibility to prepare our children for the realities of life. We all prioritize the necessities, like health, hygiene and education, but beyond that, we tend to teach what *we* value and enjoy. We love to pass down skills we learned from our parents or that we use in our professions or the hobbies we enjoy.

Does anyone enjoy making a budget? Most people just don't.

Does anyone enjoy paying bills or balancing their checking account? If so, I haven't met them.

Consider the following:

> *What is one of the most challenging parts of adult life…*
>
> *Something that you deal with or think about on a daily basis…*
>
> *For which you never received any formal education or training?*

For most of us, one answer is *money* or *managing our finances*.

Financial stress is significantly affecting the lives of Americans. A report published in January 2020 by *Thriving Wallet*, a partnership between Thrive Global and Discover, found: [1]

- Money is the No. 1 stressor in the United States.
- 90% of Americans say money has an impact on their stress level.
- 65% feel like their financial difficulties are piling up so much they can't overcome them.
- 50% of people surveyed feel unable to control important financial aspects of their lives.
- 40% wish they could have a "fresh" financial start.

- 40% say managing their money on a daily basis limits the extent to which they can enjoy their day-to-day life.
- 25% make purchases they later regret when experiencing significant stress.

We're largely left on our own to figure out basic personal financial management skills, mainly through trial and error. In too many cases, the result is stress, physical health issues, relationship problems or worse.

Let's better prepare our kids for this enormous aspect of adult life. Let's save them from the trial and error and from the stress and worry.

WHY LISTEN TO ME?

While I have years of experience in the financial services industry and a degree in finance, the only credentials that matter on this subject are the following:

1. I am the father of three daughters.
2. I designed and implemented this First Habits system with all of them.
3. Each of our daughters have now recognized the benefits of this system.
4. All three plan to use the same training for their own children.

The other relevant experience I have with this subject is actually a cautionary tale: Even with my formal education in finance, I managed to wreck my own financial situation just three years after graduating. That experience is what drove me to build this system for our daughters.

More on my story later.

THE FIRST HABITS SYSTEM

"Those most confident in their abilities to save and spend intelligently score nearly twice as high in overall well-being," according to that same January 2020 Thriving Wallet report.[2]

Confidence is defined as "a feeling of self-assurance arising from one's appreciation of one's own abilities or qualities" in the Oxford English Dictionary. Confidence is the foundation for just about every successful skill and habit we possess. The best way to develop self-assurance in an ability is by practice and learning. But where can we build financial confidence?

Schools are an important place where we build confidence, and more schools are beginning to add personal finance courses to their curriculum. But to set your child up with good money habits for life, more is needed. While schools can provide the academic education, it is up to us as parents to provide the practical training and opportunities for experience.

The First Habits system helps you do just that.

With the First Habits system, you develop a simple, practical, day-to-day plan or "Money Map" your child can use in the *real* world. They will make *real* mistakes, with *real* consequences on a small scale. This cements their learning, so that they can avoid larger mistakes with larger consequences later in life.

As your child goes through this experience, from pre-teen through college years, you will see their Money Personality and have the opportunity to shape their Money Mindset. I describe three Money Personality types: Spender, Saver and Whatever. Once you know your child's Money Personality type, the First Habits system provides guidance about areas you can emphasize and coach on. You can take the Money Personality and Money Mindset quizzes at www.FirstHabitsWin.com. The quiz results will help you form a positive and healthy Money Mindset in your child.

Your child's experience of hands-on planning and money management, along with your coaching and positive reinforcement, will help your child grow more confident about money, while developing good financial habits and a healthy, positive attitude toward financial success.

Are you ready to introduce your child to a money system that helps them make key financial decisions every day to prime them for a successful future? And can you provide a safe space within your family boundaries to allow them to *practice* this system with a certain amount of anticipated failure and success?

The First Habits system will help you prime your child for a lifetime of success by giving them an early start at making *incremental* financial decisions.

Let's face it, raising children is an expensive undertaking. We spend money on everything from school lunches to clothes and uniforms to swimming lessons. The U.S. Department of Agriculture has tracked the cost of raising a child since the 1960s, and in its most recent report noted the average middle income family spends $233,610 to raise a child from birth to age 17 (not including college costs).[3] What if, at the appropriate age, you handed the reins over to your son or daughter to manage their own day-to-day expenses, giving them a solid chance to learn about managing money before going out into the world?

That's what the First Habits system is all about.

Here's the good news: You don't need to be a finance genius to implement this system and teach your children good financial habits. All you need is a common-sense approach that's workable in everyday life. It's not rocket science. It's basic math, and it's totally doable for anyone with a fourth-grade education. The other key to success is creating the right environment to help your children develop a healthy and positive attitude toward money.

My system suggests teaching these concepts to your children in the sixth grade, or at age 12. That's when I successfully enlisted all three of our daughters. And now, as adults, they want to teach it to their children.

THREE KEYS TO SUCCESS

- Discipline
- Patience
- Persistence

Discipline

For this program to be successful for you and your family, you must be disciplined. You have to commit to funding the allowance you set up for your child. If they can't count on this commitment, it will make the process very difficult. You must also hold your child accountable. This is real money, and they must maintain their accounts and follow the system.

It seems to me that "discipline" has almost become a dirty word in our society. My daughters did not fear me, but they did *respect* me. I am not their friend, and I don't want to be. I am their father, and that goes well beyond friendship.

Once you have established a code of conduct with your children and have their respect, I have found that one of the worst punishments you can administer is to simply let your disapproval or disappointment be known.

You will know you're doing well when others tell you you're *"lucky"* to have such good kids.

It's not luck. It's consistency, firmness, fairness and a willingness to *be the parent*.

Patience

Using the First Habits system does not take a lot of time on the part of you or your child beyond the initial plan setup and tracking. However, it's not a quick fix. The lessons will be learned, and habits formed, over a period of years. The lessons may not come quickly, but they *will* happen.

You will need to display patience as your children make mistakes. This is where the real learning takes place, so mistakes and failures are actually a *good thing.*

After considerable self-reflection, I've come to believe every success I've had in my life has been born of failure. Months or years after a personal — sometimes *unnecessary* — misstep, I find that I'm able to draw a direct correlation to an achievement born of the frustration of that failure. I've come to understand it is part of my process as I navigate life's ups and downs.

Therefore, the breakdown of my ability to manage my own financial situation led me to develop a way to help myself and to teach our daughters how to manage their money starting at an early age.

"If you haven't failed yet, you haven't tried anything new." — Albert Einstein

Persistence

There were multiple times over the years when I considered scrapping the program. I questioned whether I was putting an undue burden on our children — making them responsible for planning and paying for their own expenses — and whether they were really learning anything that would help them later in life. I was even confronted by family members and other parents who thought what I was doing was a horrible mistake.

The first year I started the program with Lauren, our oldest, I was convinced that the program was turning her into a miser. I could picture her years from now, reusing the same piece of aluminum foil for 10 years.

You will likely question yourself at some point. As with any aspect of parenting — from how to get your baby to sleep to choosing how you educate your child — there's no shortage of "advice" from well-meaning family and friends. You have to choose the best path for your family. It's difficult if friends and family question how you're raising your children. And it's downright painful to watch your children struggle.

Persist. I promise, you're saving them from greater pain and struggles later in life.

MY STORY

My mother and father worked tirelessly to provide for my brother and me when we were growing up. Dad was a truck driver for a local company, and he routinely worked long hours loading trucks. Mom was the office assistant at my high school. My folks worked hard and derived their value from the work they did, not only the quantity of work but also the *quality*.

They never earned "big money," as my father would put it, but they managed their money closely, and they always provided for our family. As a result, I was given a living example of how to live within your means and the understanding that material possessions do not determine your worth.

My parents completely paid for my college education. Even with this outstanding example and head start in graduating without debt, I managed to wreck my own family's financial life within three short years. While I take full responsibility, I do believe that by simply providing for all of my needs and not *teaching me how to responsibly manage my own money,* my parents missed an opportunity that ultimately could have saved me from myself.

Just Married

After graduation, my college sweetheart, Denise, and I were soon married. Having studied finance in college, I was sure I could easily manage my first credit card.

But an introduction to the real world would soon come into play. Yes, we put our Jamaican honeymoon on credit, and yes, we needed professional attire to interview for those long-awaited and hard-earned jobs after graduation.

With plenty of room on the card, I decided Citibank obviously recognized my earning potential. In addition to those initial expenses, we found a great apartment with a pool and a gym. We completely furnished it while meeting plenty of other like-minded young professionals.

I was sure my earnings would increase, commensurate with my experience, as I continued to prove myself at work each day.

Congratulations!

But the next round of congratulations from friends and family didn't involve a promotion. Instead, we were happy to discover that we were about to become parents!

My plan for paying off Citibank was suddenly derailed by the cost of daycare, diapers and little bitty shoes that had to be replaced every six months with another pair of little bitty shoes.

By then, the list of expenditures had escalated into a $4,500 balance. (That's about $9,000 in 2020 terms.)

I convinced myself it wasn't the end of the world. I justified the expenses and continued with good intentions.

Soon after, our credit card balance rose to $6,000 ($12,000 in today's terms), and I realized I was only paying the minimum — month after month. That's when I realized the *trap* I'd created for myself and our growing family.

Runaway Train

One rainy Saturday afternoon, when I was paying the bills, the enormity of our situation hit me like a freight train. *What had I done?*

I was embarrassed. Humiliated. I felt like a hypocrite.

Worse yet, I was failing my family.

This was the kind of situation I had warned friends about. In fact, I found myself replaying moments where I'd arrogantly shared anecdotal information "from the expert" at cocktail parties.

Our debt quickly started feeling like a runaway train. If I didn't stop it now, would our balance escalate to $10K? Or $20K?

Serious Change

More than two years after graduating, getting married and beginning my new job, I was still paying for that first suit, the honeymoon and everything else I had piled on that stupid credit card.

Yes, I was making my payments on time, and we were far from financial ruin, but the burden of this debt limited our ability to save, invest or even purchase necessities.

We decided it was time to get disciplined and take control of our financial situation. We made a budget and put cash in envelopes for each major category. Rent, fuel, groceries, everything had an envelope.

I have vivid memories of spending hours working on the budget and writing the largest check I could to Citibank every month. It wasn't easy. One night, Denise came to me crying; she didn't have enough gas in her car to get to work and the fuel envelope was empty. Thankfully, I had started another emergency envelope that I raided to solve the no-gas problem.

We made a lot of sacrifices while working our way out of the debt we had built. Those memories remain with me to this day, and the experience continues to influence my spending habits.

As a student of finance, I am an advocate of the appropriate use of debt. For example, the use of debt in business can accelerate growth. In purchasing a home, it can save you thousands of dollars in rent payments. But it can also handcuff you and severely limit your options if used inappropriately.

Early Lessons

Growing up, my parents had been the model of frugality and a golden example of how to live within one's means. They had made significant sacrifices to pay for my college education, and in three short years I had completely blown the opportunity of living debt free.

I didn't share my situation with anyone but Denise, for fear that I'd be found out for the poser I was. So, I kept it to myself and focused my energy on paying off the credit card balance.

I felt like a fraud.

Everything Is Relative

About the same time that Denise and I were trying to get our financial life back together, my college friend "Joe" was back in town and stopped by to visit.

Joe and I both graduated with degrees in finance. While I stayed in Kansas, Joe landed a dream job on Wall Street straight out of school. He was the smartest person I have ever known, and he taught me that everything is relative.

I talked with Joe every few months by phone. He told me stories about life in the fast lane, including his latest purchases. In turn, I would share stories of 2 a.m. feedings and the outrageous cost of daycare.

Even though I thought Joe would understand my situation — and I knew I needed someone to talk to — I was too embarrassed to share my recent personal financial epiphanies.

We sat down at the kitchen table, and as he drank his first beer, Joe's eyes widened with excitement as he recounted stories about his timeshare, custom-made suits, exotic trips and his new BMW.

I felt like such a dud listening to him. I was still living in an apartment and worried about paying for diapers and formula.

Listening to Joe's stories, I felt like I didn't measure up. In fact, I was downright humiliated with my situation.

After a few beers, Joe loosened up a little and spoke openly about his debt. He told me he had accumulated a $50,000 balance on his Visa.

I remember thinking, *Are you just looking for ways to burn through cash? Why would you have $50,000 in credit card debt if you are making enough to buy new BMWs and custom-made suits?*

He had a reason for everything, and it all boiled down to keeping up appearances and measuring his self-worth on someone else's scale.

He shared that he'd recently quit his job, but he didn't seem worried about it. He was confident he'd get a job at a local brokerage firm. Joe was supremely confident in his ability to earn, so spending was a non-issue to him.

The next day, as I was rocking Lauren with "Barney" on TV in the background, I realized I didn't have the right to be judgmental. We were both being irresponsible, just in different ways.

Everything is relative.

Over the next several years, I kept in touch with Joe. He worked at the local brokerage firm, met the love of his life and got married. Denise and I attended his wedding, and he seemed happier than ever. After the wedding, he told me he owed Visa $75,000, and then he and his new wife moved to the West Coast.

Before talking with Joe, I had always planned on being able to earn my way out of trouble. While I was budgeting and being more disciplined about my spending, I was also thinking about the next raise or bonus or the next job. I finally came to the realization that regardless of your income, you can be undisciplined and have financial problems, whether the problem is $5,000 on a credit card or $75,000.

Everything truly is relative.

While I've experienced dozens of other hard lessons over the years, my own failure and the lesson I learned from Joe have stood out as the most impactful, and they are the reason I taught our daughters the system that evolved into First Habits, which I outline in the following chapters.

SECTION TWO

What Is Your Money Mindset?

Never spend your money before you have earned it.

— Thomas Jefferson, Founding Father and Third President of the United States

IDENTIFY YOUR MONEY MINDSET

Two key factors influence how we handle our financial affairs.

1. First is the influence that comes from our environment: What we learned from our parents growing up and what we see and hear from close friends and relatives today. This is our Money Mindset and what I'll talk about in this section of the book.

2. The second key factor is your Money Personality, which I'll discuss in the next section.

This section on Money Mindset is largely influenced by the book "Wired For Wealth," by Brad Klontz, Psy.D., Ted Klontz, Ph.D., and Rick Kahler, CFP°. I share some of the teaching directly from the book, but I highly recommend reading this book yourself to gain a more complete understanding of what the authors call "money scripts" and how they influence our decisions. In some cases, such money scripts can drive us to subconsciously sabotage our own financial success.

Money Mindsets are formed and influenced by our environment. We each have a financial comfort zone that has both a floor and a ceiling on wealth and income. For example, Dave and Mary live in a middle-class suburban neighborhood. Their friends and neighbors live in the same or similar neighborhoods, shop in the same stores and share a similar lifestyle. While their incomes and net worth may vary significantly, they all fit in the same financial comfort zone. To validate their comfort zone, they may share beliefs with one another that others just above their comfort zone are greedy and others just below their comfort zone are lazy. These are what are referred to as money scripts in "Wired For Wealth."

Money scripts can be positive or negative. The examples "greedy" and "lazy" are negative money scripts, and they influence your Money Mindset. If Dave and Mary get near the upper end of their comfort zone for any reason, they will have to deal, at least subconsciously, with the idea of their current group of friends and family viewing them as greedy. Their friends and family may even chastise their success, even if in a joking tone. "I see the For Sale sign in your yard, Dave. Too good for our little neighborhood, are we?"

A Money Mindset is enormously powerful and can even cause people to avoid too much success or the accumulation of wealth. A negative Money Mindset might cause a person to spend impulsively or invest in a high-risk business venture or other means of squandering wealth to remain in one's financial comfort zone.

A negative Money Mindset about the floor of your financial comfort zone can also be a bad thing, especially with kids. Consider Sandra. She is from an upper-middle-class family and has just graduated from college and landed her first job. Her parents paid for college and gave Sandra spending money as well. Sandra's Money Mindset was largely influenced by her family, so she identifies with their financial comfort zone. This includes eating at nice restaurants and wearing expensive clothes.

Sandra's first job is exciting and offers her a ton of potential to grow and earn more, but her starting salary is entry level. Based on her income, she should be in a lower comfort zone than her parents, but if her Money Mindset is negative about those in a lower comfort zone, she may make poor money choices to remain in her parents' comfort zone. She may take on credit card debt or keep buying clothes she cannot afford on her salary.

Equally as powerful as a negative Money Mindset is a positive Money Mindset. Dr. Brad Klontz and his associates identify five money scripts that promote wealth from a survey they conducted. They refer to these as "wealth scripts."

1. It is important to save for a rainy day.
2. Giving money to others is something people should do.
3. Money buys freedom.
4. I have to work hard to be sure I have enough money.
5. I deserve money.

These five beliefs were strongly associated with higher income and net worth. The first wealth script explained 75% of the difference between those who were wealthy and those who were not.

The fifth wealth script reminds me of a poem by Jessie B. Rittenhouse, "My Wage."

My Wage

> *I bargained with life for a penny,*
> *And life would pay no more,*
> *However I begged at evening*
> *When I counted my scanty store.*
>
> *For life is a just employer,*
> *He gives you what you ask,*
> *But once you have set the wages,*
> *Why, then you must bear the task.*
>
> *I worked for a menial's hire,*
> *Only to learn, dismayed,*
> *That any wage I had asked of life,*
> *Life would have willingly paid.*

When I read this poem, I think of some of the most talented artists I know. They consistently undervalue and therefore underprice their work. You must believe that your work has value and that you deserve to be paid for it.

Think about how much this belief alone could impact your son or daughter's earning power.

Have you ever heard, or maybe you've said it yourself, "No way one person is worth that much money"? This is usually in reference to a public figure like an athlete or artist, but it could also be about a CEO or a highly compensated person in any role. Statements like this can seed a subconscious mindset in a child when they hear a parent say this. It may cause them to avoid earning a higher salary for fear of falling out of favor with a respected parent.

YOUR MISSION, SHOULD YOU CHOOSE TO ACCEPT IT

Your mission is to identify and purposefully develop your child's Money Mindset.

As parents, we are the most influential people in our children's lives. Yes, even as they get older and it seems like they are more inclined to do the opposite of what we advise. If we aren't consciously working to provide the best influence and advice, there are plenty of alternative influences competing for our children's attention.

Today we have thousands of friends on Facebook, Instagram, Snapchat and Twitter, and we get notified every time one of them goes somewhere cool or buys something new. We come to the conclusion that everyone else is taking a vacation, so why shouldn't we?

We are comparing our lives to the very best individual moments of thousands of people. The fact that friend #739 went to Europe on vacation; friend #137 just purchased a new home; and friend #412 just purchased a luxury car is only part of the story they post online. What we don't see are the years of savings and discipline that went into that dream vacation or the unsustainable debt that car purchase contributed to that may ultimately lead to bankruptcy.

While comparison is a downside of social media, equally detrimental is the negativity on social media. This can be a big influence on a child's Money Mindset. Imagine your 14-year-old daughter sees her friend group shame or attack someone on social media for the clothes they wear or where they live. Your daughter's mindset is being shaped — either to view wealth and expensive clothes or homes as a negative, in which case she may subconsciously avoid the accumulation of wealth, or to view less affluent clothing styles or living arrangements as a negative, in which case she may pursue spending beyond her means.

As a parent, you still have more influence than her friend group. While she likes her friends, she respects you. You have molded her values and instilled a sense of right and wrong in her since she was a baby. She doesn't have to *like* you as well as her friends to still *respect* you. You have the power to counter all of the outside influences to create a healthy and positive Money Mindset.

As a father, I worked hard to make sure my daughters derived their value from who they were and not *what they owned*. The brand of backpack, jeans or shoes has absolutely nothing to do with the value of the person wearing them.

In seventh grade, having the right brand of jeans may seem like a life or death issue, socially speaking. If you allow your child to make the decision about whether they use 100% of their monthly income to buy social status, they will ultimately learn a valuable lesson.

By the way, there is a very slim chance of teaching your children this lesson by simply *telling* them. Although they may obey, they have not *learned* the lesson. Some things must be learned by experience.

Your child will be empowered by having a choice but will be constrained at the same time. If they buy the jeans, it means they can't go to the movies because they don't have the money.

Depending on their Money Personality, expect the jeans to win out in the beginning, maybe even on multiple occasions.

WATCH WHAT YOU ARE SAYING

I have witnessed the fear and anxiety that many people have when it comes to managing money. I believe a lot of this is caused by the junk we hear about money from an early age.

Have you heard these sayings? Or perhaps repeated them yourself?

"Money is the root of all evil."
"Money can't buy happiness."

"Money burns a hole in your pocket."

Financial success is often associated with greed, materialism, the mistreatment of others, lying, cheating and even criminal behavior.

While I will readily admit that I have seen these behaviors among financially successful people, I have also seen them among those who have *not* been financially successful.

Additionally, I have seen generosity, honest dealing and downright heroic acts from people of all economic means. These old clichés can become manufactured reasons to account for an *unwillingness* to take control and be accountable for your own success.

Goodness or evil is *in your heart,* and good people do good things with their money, time and talents. Money truly cannot "buy" happiness, *but poverty does not ensure it either!*

We all need to be conscious of what we are repeating to ourselves and to our children through our actions and comments.

SECTION THREE

Spenders, Savers and Whatevers

Empty pockets never held anyone back. Only empty heads and empty hearts can do that.

– Norman Vincent Peale, minister and author of "The Power of Positive Thinking"

YOUR MONEY PERSONALITY

The second key factor that influences how we handle our financial affairs is our Money Personality.

We all have unique, hardwired personality traits. Studies show pain and pleasure centers in our brains react differently in each of us and govern our spending and saving habits — even when we know better.

As I have researched this subject, I have found numerous personality types identified. Of course, Saver and Spender are common, but others include Shopper, Debtor, Investor, Hoarder, Avoider, Amasser, Money Monk, Status Seeker, Free Spirit, Selfless Spender, Security Seeker, Risk Taker, Worrier and Flyer. While I can understand the reason for each of these personality types to be individually identified, I believe most are secondary to one of three core personality traits.

I believe one simple question defines your Money Personality: When you have money, do you spend it, save it or do you avoid dealing with it or just not care that much about it?

Note there are positive *and* negative attributes to each personality type.

The Saver

Having cash in the bank or experiencing significant savings on a product or service brings Savers pleasure. The victory of a good bargain makes everyone feel good, but Savers feel the rush even more because it's a relief from the discomfort of needing to spend. Studies have found that the *discomfort* is actually the trigger. An area in the brain called the insula is stimulated when we experience something unpleasant; for Savers, spending is unpleasant. They generally avoid spending, or at least look for the very best deal, to avoid the unpleasant experience. Researchers concluded that people who have more insula activity in their brains are more likely to be Savers, and those with less tend to be Spenders.[4]

The Spender

The decision or act of making a purchase releases dopamine, a neurotransmitter responsible for feelings of pleasure, in the brain. Spenders get more of a dopamine release when making a purchase, thus overriding any discomfort.[5]

Savers experience more pain and less pleasure than Spenders when making a purchase. Conversely, Spenders get more pleasure and experience less pain than Savers when making a purchase.

The Whatever

The third Money Mindset I have titled "Whatever." I chose this label because my youngest daughter truly did not care. (More on her Money Personality later.) We are all hardwired to do what comes naturally to us, even the Whatever personality.

Often misunderstood, the Whatever personality avoids making financial decisions. Money may be intimidating for them, or money may just not be a big deal to them. They aren't triggered by it the way Spenders and Savers are. Maybe the dopamine release and the insula stimulation cancel each other out. Whatevers either *really* don't care or they may be avoiding dealing with a situation they find unpleasant or even intimidating.

Multiple Personalities

We all display traits from multiple Money Personalities. Spenders save and Savers spend, and we all just Whatever sometimes, but we each have a dominant Money Personality. My objective in identifying the dominant personality is to tailor the learning and environmental influences to the needs of each individual.

I'm the type of person who learns best from making my own mistakes, and I wanted to give our daughters the opportunities to make mistakes within a controlled environment. I wanted to remove the fear and anxiety of dealing with money to allow them to learn from making small mistakes early in life rather than larger ones later.

When I began the deliberate process of teaching our daughters about money, one of my objectives was to help them form good habits. I thought if I could teach them good basic habits about spending within their means, balancing their checking account and other simple tasks, I could embed this into their financial foundation.

I can see that my efforts helped our daughters, but I failed early on to consider one key aspect, their Money Personality.

We are all born with a Money Personality. Even after being raised in the same environment and participating in the same First Habits system, each of our three daughters manages their money quite differently.

I didn't consider Money Personality as I started this system with our oldest. Although we tailored the specifics of the system to each of our daughters, the idea of a hardwired Money Personality did not occur to me until much later. In fact, I started my research on this topic in search of an answer to why our daughters were each so different.

While there were positive outcomes from adjusting the system to fit each of our daughters, I know now that there was much more I could have done. As I share stories about our daughters' experiences throughout this book, I've also incorporated some additional simple tips and instruction to help better manage those emotional triggers. Watch for the "If I Had It To Do Over" sections.

REAL STORIES

Lauren (The Saver Personality)

Our oldest daughter, **Lauren,** is a hardwired Saver, even though she doesn't have the conservative personality you might expect. An outgoing personality who is often the life of the party, she is also extremely caring, fun to be around and would do anything for anyone.

As a pre-teen, when it came to money, she was motivated by watching her savings account increase over time. Lauren decided very quickly, after confirming she wouldn't have to pay for bread and sandwich ingredients, that she would save money by taking her lunch to school rather than paying for school lunch.

Savers may avoid spending money at all costs. For example, Denise and I realized we would need to define some purchases as mandatory for Lauren. One example was dress clothes to wear to weddings, funerals, church, etc. — purchases she would have chosen to avoid otherwise. Once we communicated which expenses were mandatory, Lauren agreed and was fine with it.

Savers need to learn to prioritize what's important to them as well as some of life's indulgences. One of the best ways to do this is to earmark money for specific purchases. Depending on the individual, this may just be for large purchases like a car or a vacation. In some cases, it may be necessary to allocate funds for such categories as clothes and groceries to help manage the emotions of the Saver.

Savers see savings account dollars as their safety net, not to be touched unless it's a true emergency. If they have a separate vacation account, it's much easier for them to spend the money for its intended purpose. In Lauren's case, she had money in her plan for dress clothes, and once she understood this was a mandatory expense, she didn't experience the pain associated with the purchase.

* * * * * * * * * * * * * * * * * *

Hayley (The Spender Personality)

Our middle daughter, **Hayley**, is quite different from her older sister. Hayley is a perfectionist and a hardwired Spender. She is academically gifted and driven in everything she undertakes. Hayley is purposeful in action and responds well to incentives and rewards.

When it came to money, she was motivated by a desire to experience life. Concerts, ballgames, dinner with friends, clothes and so on were all enticing to her. Her positive energy and fun personality attract people to her, which leads to endless invitations. Saying no is not an option for Hayley.

This is typical of most Spenders, but it can also come with frequent buyer's remorse and a lack of security in the form of savings.

As a Spender myself, it was hard for me to identify ways to help Hayley manage her Spender personality. She has done some things on her own that are perfect for us Spenders. She has activated an option with her bank that rounds all purchases she makes with her debit card up to the nearest dollar and then adds that amount to a savings account. She also has savings taken directly from her paycheck and deposited into a savings account. And she has managed her online banking dashboard to hide her savings account, so she isn't tempted to dip into it.

* * * * * * * * * * * * * * * * * *

Anna (The Whatever Personality)

Our youngest daughter, **Anna**, is a hardwired Whatever. She's cool with most things, though she has strong opinions regarding the things she's passionate about, including politics, morality and religion. Oh, and makeup.

Her personal belief system is deeply rooted in faith, yet there are other things she doesn't care about, and money just happens to be one of them. To Anna, it wouldn't matter if she had $80 or $80,000 in her account. It took me a long time to truly understand that this was *actually* the case. I was convinced she was just not sharing her true feelings.

The biggest challenge for someone with the Whatever Money Personality is that they have a tendency to just not deal with things, like paying bills or keeping their bank account balance positive. I think the practices Anna learned in the First Habits system would have been much harder for her to develop at an older age and with her own money.

Developing a routine can help the Whatever personality: for example, paying bills at the same time every week or month and developing the discipline to make a budget and track spending and saving.

MANAGING *YOUR* MONEY PERSONALITY

As I mentioned earlier, I'm a Spender. Even though my parents modeled disciplined savings and lived within their means, those behaviors did not align with my core personality. I give my parents credit for being a great example, but I had to learn the hard way.

Denise, on the other hand, is a Saver. She is also a bit of a Whatever, as she doesn't want to deal with financial matters. Denise was raised by a single mother in a home where frugality and saving was a requirement. Denise's mom also paid for her college education, so both of us graduated without any debt or student loans.

We have both worked to manage our Money Personalities and find a balance. For me, that meant planning for expenses, having an established savings routine and agreeing on larger expenditures ahead of time.

We shouldn't expect to change the Money Personality of a Saver, Spender or Whatever, but learning to manage the negative and harmful aspects of a particular personality early in life can have an enormous effect on your child's happiness and contentment over time.

SECTION FOUR

The First Habits System

It's the little details that are vital. Little things make big things happen.

– John Wooden, record–setting UCLA basketball coach

GETTING STARTED
WITH THE FIRST HABITS SYSTEM

As complicated and scary as they may seem, the basic concepts of planning, tracking and managing your money aren't difficult to understand. It's a combination of basic math (simple addition and subtraction) and simple discipline. Both are much easier to teach — and learn! — at a young age.

Additionally, there is a strong emotional and psychological component to dealing with money issues that I believe should be taught at home. Once you know your child's Money Personality —expect each child to be different — you can tailor a program just for them.

Here's the best part: Your child's education will come from practical experience. Some of this may actually result in failure — and that's OK. Failure is how most of us learn!

Failure is not a bad word to me. In fact, I consider it an integral component of success. Failure is evidence that you have actually *tried*. The only way to avoid failure is to never try anything, to never take a chance.

I should know. I was the stubborn kid who had to learn everything the hard way. My parents would teach me great life lessons, and I would go right out and do the opposite. I had to learn by experience, making my own mistakes.

Knowing this as a parent, I wanted to provide a controlled environment for our daughters so they could make mistakes and learn those same lessons on a small scale, with a safety net. Additionally, I wanted to remove the angst of dealing with money, starting at an early age.

You will implement the First Habits system with three simple steps that set your child up to budget, plan and track their expenses:

Step 1: Prepare a Plan or Money Map with your child

Step 2: Open your child's accounts and teach them to track and balance the account

Step 3: Explain the system to your child

That's it!

These new habits and skills you'll teach your children will give them an advantage when they face future financial milestones, including getting their first credit card, buying a car, paying college expenses, building their credit score and being cautious of debt.

Throughout this section I will refer to and include screenshots of an app I developed to help you manage the First Habits system with your child. The app is called Cabbage and is available on the App Store for Apple users or Google Play for Android users. I also have a downloadable Excel planning spreadsheet on the First Habits Win website, www.FirstHabitsWin.com. The downloads and app are free and should make this system easier to start and manage with your child.

STEP 1 — THE MONEY MAP

In the First Habits system, I have avoided the term "budget" because of the negative associations to the word. Instead I use the term "plan" or "Money Map." It's easy to explain to a child that you're creating a plan or mapping out the sources and uses of money. I want to explain the different philosophies and what we use in the First Habits system, then we will retire the word "budget" for the rest of the book.

Budget Philosophy

There are several types of personal budgets. The First Habits system uses a combination of Savings First and Zero-Based budgets. Following is an overview of the four most common personal budgets.

Left-Over Budget

Also referred to as Spending First budget. With this method, you make sure you can cover your essential needs and commitments and then try to control discretionary spending after those are met. At the end of the month, put whatever is left over into savings.

I don't recommend this method. Spenders will almost never have anything left over to save, and Savers will deny themselves too much.

Savings First Budget

As the name implies, this method starts with savings. This can be a percentage or a fixed dollar amount, but the idea is to "pay yourself first." Once you have covered your savings requirement, you're free to spend the rest as you desire.

By satisfying the savings first, you limit yourself from overspending or overcommitting on a car or house payment.

Zero-Based Budget

With this method, you plan for every dollar of income you earn. This includes saving, spending, charitable giving and investing. You can be as comprehensive or nonspecific as you want.

I recommend a few broad categories to keep it simple.

50/30/20 Budget

This is a popular budget method that prescribes the following split for after-tax income.

50% – Needs (examples: housing, utilities, food)

30% – Wants (examples: entertainment, travel)

20% – Savings

These are broad categories, and I'm sure we all define wants and needs differently. For lower-income families this may be difficult, but it would be a good goal to shoot for as income increases and debt gets paid off.

For people who want more detailed budgeting guidance, the following categories and percentages are common.

- 10% – Giving
- 10% – Savings
- 10% - 15% – Food
- 5% - 10% – Utilities
- 25% – Housing
- 10% – Transportation
- 5% - 10% – Health
- 10% - 25% – Insurance
- 5% - 10% – Recreation
- 5% - 10% – Personal
- 5% - 10% – Miscellaneous

To prepare a plan for your child, you will need to do some prep work. Start this step by adding up what you have spent on your child over the previous year. Include clothes, sports, school expenses and gifts, just to name a few. The best way to do this would be to track and record all expenses from their 11th birthday on by going back through your bank account, credit card statements or checkbook register, adding up everything spent over the course of the year.

You can download a planning spreadsheet template at www.FirstHabitsWin.com. With this planning tool, you enter income first. Once income is entered, you can determine how much will go to savings each month. I've labeled the first savings line item "Pay Myself First." This can be used to establish an emergency fund of three to six months of income. Once that is accomplished, this line item can be used to add to a car fund or other savings goal. Use this tool to plan the entire year's income, savings, expenses and charitable gifts. Once you have this complete, you can set up the individual tracking accounts in the Cabbage app.

The app is broken down into five categories.

- **Expected Income:** This category would include income from an allowance or a part-time job that is predictable and reoccurring.
- **Other Income:** This is for gifts and income from babysitting or other periodic or unpredictable sources.
- **Must Pay:** This category is for both savings and required expenses. For the savings, it is paid out of a checking account to a savings account. For expenses for adults, it would include rent or mortgage, utilities and loan payments. For kids, this would include music lessons or subscriptions and could include paying Mom and Dad for a cell phone. These are normal reoccurring expenses. This is also the category in which to set up a charitable gift if you want to make it a routine for your child.
- **Can Spend:** This is for discretionary expenses like clothes, entertainment or eating out. While some of these expenses may be necessities, like clothes, they are not contractual obligations or routine and reoccurring.
- **Future Expense:** This category is for larger expenses like a sports team fee or uniform costs due at the beginning of a season. I also put gifts in this category so there will be money set aside for Christmas and birthdays. This should also be transferred to a separate account to accumulate over time and then transferred back to the checking account when the expense is due.

The Cabbage app lets you set up your plan using a wizard that walks you through creating accounts for Income, Savings, Charity and Expenses.

Overview screen shows month-to-date savings, income, spending, and charitable giving. It also gives a "cushion" showing net earning and spending.

Customize accounts for your specific needs.

Easily keep control of discretionary spending
with real time per week and per day available
calculations.

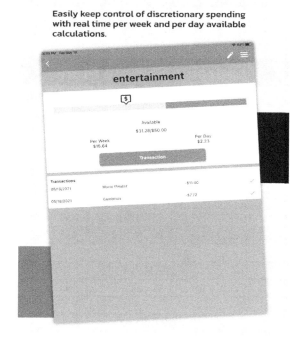

As you do this, you will notice certain expenses will be concentrated in certain months, with no expenses in other months. This will take some planning and saving, so it is important to be as accurate as possible with the timing of these expenses.

In Lauren's Sample Budget, notice her sports fees are only due in April, but they are a large amount. The way to approach a situation like this is to teach your child to begin saving ahead. If they save an equal amount each month, they will have the amount they need when the expense is due. Both the app and the spreadsheet template help with this using the Future Expense category. You will just need to divide the total amount of the one-time expense by 12 to get the set-aside expense total for each month.

For the sports fees in Lauren's Sample Plan, the total yearly cost is $1,050. When Lauren saved $87.50 each month (over 12 months), she had the money set aside for this expense when it came due in April.

When you are first starting this system, you will need to plan ahead for these types of expenses, so you're not blindsided later.

Lauren's Sample Plan				
Category	**Source**	**Frequency**	**Amount**	**Due Date**
INCOME				
Allowance	Mom & Dad	Monthly	$400	1st of month
Babysitting	Various	Weekly	$20	1st of month
Concession stand	Ball Assn.	Weekly	$15	1st of month
SAVINGS				
Pay myself first	10%	Monthly	$54	1st of month
Car fund	½ cost of car	Monthly	$50	1st of month
CHARITY				
St. Theresa	Weekly gift	Weekly	$5	2nd of month
EXPENSES				
	Monthly set aside?			**Month due**
Clothes/ shoes	No	Monthly	$75	
School supplies/fees	Yes	Annual	$25	Aug.
School lunch	No	Monthly	$30.25	
Sports fees/ equipment/ uniforms	Yes	Annual	$87.50	April
Piano lessons	No	Weekly	$15	
Entertainment	No	Monthly	$75	
Gifts	Yes	Monthly	$25	Jan.
Misc.		Monthly	$38.25	

I started our kids with a monthly allowance plus an additional one-time allowance that would cover those non-recurring expenses with a normal planning pattern. In the case of Lauren's $1,050 sports fees due in April, if I had started her on the program in November, for example, I would have initially given her an extra $612.50 toward this cost. Then she would save $87.50 a month for the next five months ($437.50) to have the full $1,050 by April.

$612.50

+ $437.50

$1,050.00

Additionally, I would need to give her another one-time startup allowance for school supplies and gifts. By the next year, Lauren would be able to cover all expenses on her own by saving the set-aside amount each month.

Hey, I never said this part was fun. The hard work behind the scenes never is.

Large expenses can be managed in the Cabbage App by scheduling the expense item for a future date. Cabbage will calculate the amount to be set aside each month until the expense is due and add that amount to the monthly plan.

Add Future Expense Account

Account Name
Softball Fees and Uniform

Target Amount to Collect ($)
1050.00

○ Months to collect:

◉ One Time. Collect by:

04/01/2022

Confirm   Cancel

Softball Fees and Uniform

Month Remaining	Total Remaining
-$0.00/$87.50	$962.50/$1,050.00

Transaction

Transactions

05/01/2021 Set aside for Chili   -$87.50   ✓
Pepper's 2022

Future Expense set-up wizard

Future Expense tracking for monthly set aside and total future expense

Other tricky plan items are the ones that vary each month. For example, school lunch cost changes from month to month. I calculated the cost based on the number of school days in each month, multiplied by the cost of a single school lunch.

This school lunch plan item also has months during the summer where there is no expense. You can treat this the same way we did the sports fees and have your child save an equal amount over 12 months; you will just need to make sure they will have enough to cover those more expensive months.

You should also consider the potential for new expenses you did not have in the previous year as you develop the budget. At the age of 12, many children move from elementary to middle school, and with that comes more expenses associated with social events and sports, just to name a few. The school calendar can be a big help in planning for these things when you are building your budget.

For our daughters, I gave them a fixed allowance every month. I wanted them to learn to plan and save for future expenses with a fixed amount of money each month. For Lauren's plan, these variable expenses were school supplies, school lunches, school fees and sports fees. Then there are unknown expenses like clothes/shoes, entertainment and gifts. While the plan is the same each month, the expenditures will vary from month to month. Use the Can Spend category for these expenses in Cabbage.

I also included a Miscellaneous line item in the plan. This is for allowance that is not earmarked for any planned expense. I do this with our personal plan too, and I use it as a cushion for unexpected or unplanned expenses.

Watch what your children do with these funds. If they spend the entire amount every month, they probably have a Spender Money Personality. If it goes straight into savings, they likely have a Saver Money Personality. If the money just sits there and they don't do anything with it, they may fit in the Whatever Money Personality.

Detours and Roadblocks

As part of your plan, you will want to set aside some money for deviations. Your child could have a growth spurt, outgrowing clothes every six months, or have an opportunity to travel with their school and have additional fees to pay. The miscellaneous line item or savings category won't always cover these expenses.

For us, one example of this was when Hayley was invited to be part of a national youth leadership organization and attend the 2012 presidential inauguration in Washington, D.C. We didn't want her to miss the opportunity, and Denise and I happily paid for the trip.

STEP 2 — OPEN THEIR ACCOUNTS

I took each of our daughters to the bank to open accounts on their 12th birthday. It was a rite of passage that I believe all parents should consider.

As you take your child to the bank to open their checking account and obtain their debit card, be sure to help them open a savings account at the same time. (That piggy bank doesn't earn interest!) Require that they put a percentage in savings every month to help them form a healthy habit of *paying yourself first*. (I recommend 10%; it's easy to calculate quickly, when moving income to savings. It's small enough to not make an enormous dent in their allowance but will accumulate nicely over time.)

This savings will act as a safety net because — as they will soon learn — there's often a difference, a time lag, between their account's *online balance* (what's been posted) and the *actual balance* (what's been spent).

Open accounts in your child's name and add both parents as well. While I developed and implemented this system with the girls, Denise played a huge part in teaching and helping them. Be sure to also set up online banking, with alerts, to monitor any issues. Your child will likely love the ease of having their accounts tied together through online banking — a luxury we never had at their age!

Show your child how to record deposits and withdrawals and how to balance the account. If you are using the Cabbage app, there are tools to help with tracking to the plan. You will still need to record transactions for the bank account as well. The following screenshots show recording an income transaction and a savings transaction in the app.

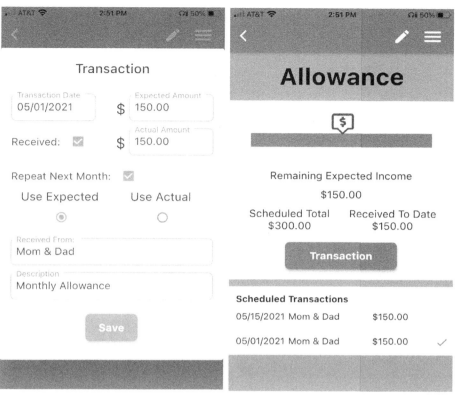

Income set up wizard   *Income/ Allowance tracking screen*

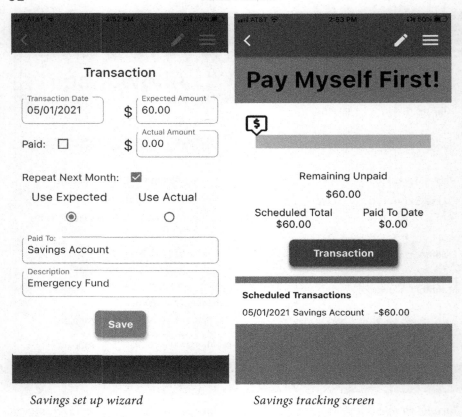

Savings set up wizard   Savings tracking screen

STEP 3 — EXPLAIN THE SYSTEM TO YOUR CHILD

Next, you will need to sit down with your child and explain the plan you've set and how they will balance their bank account, as this process can be intimidating. Start with the savings and emphasize the need to prioritize paying yourself first. Explain that a lot of adults' financial problems begin with an unexpected expense that they couldn't cover because they didn't have adequate savings in an emergency fund. Then, walk through all of the expenses, how you came to the numbers and why they need to save for things like sports fees or items that only come due once or twice a year.

I would suggest using this opportunity to boost their confidence as much as possible. You will also want to let them know that you *expect them to make mistakes* as part of the learning experience.

For example, you could say: *Robert, we are very proud of you, and we think you are ready to have your own checking and savings account and debit cards. We have put together a plan of the things you will need to pay for, and we will give you the money to pay for your expenses, but it will be your responsibility to follow the plan and pay for them on time.*

We will help you with this until you get comfortable enough to do it on your own. Many adults have trouble managing the money, so we don't expect you to be perfect. If you make a mistake, we will help you correct it.

In the beginning, we provided a monthly allowance for our daughters in the form of a check. As the girls got older and more comfortable with the system, I scheduled an automatic electronic monthly payment direct to their accounts.

As you introduce the system, you may experience a range of reactions from your child.

So, how did our three daughters fare when they were introduced to the system on their 12th birthdays? I had one daughter, Lauren, who was excited and couldn't stop smiling and another, Hayley, who was so scared she was almost physically sick. My youngest, Anna, was Miss No Reaction — Whatever. I am not sure if being third and seeing her sisters' experiences had any impact, but she took it in stride.

Even though it's obvious, I'd like to say there are no winners or losers in the First Habits system. This is all about providing our children with practical money management experience before going out into the real world. Because each of our daughters falls into different Money Personality categories — Saver, Spender and Whatever — each reacted differently.

You will likely notice that your children all have their own Money Personality, and you will want to treat them individually, aligned with their own personalities.

WHAT YOU'LL NEED

Remember, the most important part of the First Habits system is having the discipline to allow your child to fail in order to learn. It's an essential tool for them, and it's also the hardest part. You will guide them, but don't control the experience.

Let them overdraw their account or, later when they have a credit card, charge something they can't immediately pay off, so they experience those stumbles and the emotions that go with them. Then feel free to discuss how it happened and what their options are to correct the mistake and make sure it doesn't happen again. Let them work their way out of the problem.

After all, isn't that how you've learned?

The worst thing you can do is *buy* them out of their problem. Trust me, this may be your first instinct.

The good news? You won't need anything fancy to prepare your teen for the First Habits system, and the tools are all free. The tracking can be done with the free planning spreadsheet on the website, www.FirstHabitsWin.com, or in the free Cabbage app, or even with notebooks and check registers if you prefer. The Money Mindset and Money Personality quizzes will help tailor the system to fit your child's unique personality and help you manage how you are influencing their views and beliefs toward money and wealth.

Here are the tools you can use to teach your child the First Habits system:

- Download the tools for free at www.FirstHabitsWin.com.
- Take the quiz to identify your Money Mindset, which is also free at www.FirstHabitsWin.com and on the Cabbage app.

- Check out the Cabbage app, for Android and Apple phones, available on the App Store and Google Play. The app provides a plan setup wizard, tracking and notifications for both parents and children.
- Use online banking to help your child balance their savings and checking accounts.
- Create your own trackers with a notebook or Excel spreadsheets.

PARENT MINDSET

As you practice the system, it's important to **be aware of your own mindset as a parent.**

Here are three tips I want you to remember as you embark on this journey with your child:

- **Ignore the opinions of others.** Don't be swayed by family and friends who don't understand the concept of the First Habits system. You may be ridiculed for not helping your child in ways others deem appropriate. Stay strong. These lessons are for the *long game.* I've learned that it is *less compassionate* to constantly hand over money every time your teen asks — or bail them out in the midst of this program. By doing this, you have allowed them to endure the pain without any benefit of learning. **Persistence and discipline are two of the keys to success identified earlier.**

- **Spend time teaching.** Be patient in showing your children the basics. Start by helping them set up their first checking and savings accounts. Teach your child the specific tasks of depositing, balancing and planning spending, but remember most of their learning will come from experience on their part. You will need to be prepared to guide and coach them as issues come up. **Patience is another one of the keys to success identified earlier.**

- **Remember, your history doesn't matter.** The money problems you've had in your life should not be treated like a pre-existing condition. If you haven't practiced any of the disciplines in this book, it's OK. By teaching your children these basic principles, you will save them years of stress and anxiety. You may even adopt some of these disciplines yourself to improve your own money management skills.

The plan works as your child's personal GPS for income and expenditures. But this money map doesn't always show the hidden detours and roadblocks that will inevitably surface. So, we will also prepare for these incidentals with a backup plan.

Throughout the book, I have included lessons that were important to our family that I think will help you along the way. I also included tips and stories to prepare you for some of the surprises you may encounter.

The "If I Had It To Do Over" sections in the book will give you some insights about how you may want to change the system to fit your needs. I strongly encourage you to treat this as a general outline and alter the First Habits system to fit your specific needs and values.

BE PREPARED

The reason I started the program when our daughters turned 12 years old is because younger children learn more quickly and easily than teenagers, young adults and adults. Also, spending habits are formed early, and by age 12 children are preparing to enter middle school.

In middle school, clothes, brands and style become a larger influence. I didn't want our daughters to define their worth based on the brand they were wearing. Anything you can teach your children is valuable; we chose to focus on the basics of personal financial management.

Many people have praised my efforts with the First Habits system, but an equal number have criticized me. I have been accused of making our daughters grow up too quickly, of putting too much emphasis on money, and of being strict, or even mean, for not buying them what they wanted.

To be honest, I questioned myself on multiple occasions but at no time more seriously than during the Broken Knee Incident.

Lauren was attending a birthday party sleepover at a friend's house when we received one of those calls that every parent dreads: Your daughter is hurt. The call was from her friend's mother telling us Lauren had hurt her knee. It was pretty bad. We rushed over to discover her knee was swollen to three times its normal size, and she could not bend it or bear any weight.

We loaded her in the back seat of the car with her leg elevated and iced it for the ride to the emergency room. Lauren is tough and has an extremely high pain tolerance. She rarely cries, and when she does, you know it's serious.

We asked how she hurt her knee and how bad the pain was. She explained that she was riding a scooter down a steep hill and had stepped off to slow down.

Then, Lauren asked a question that almost ripped my heart out. "Dad, do I have to pay to get my knee fixed?"

"OH MY GOD, NO!" I answered. "We will always take care of you, Lauren. You're on our insurance plan. Don't worry about it, Honey. The 'system' is just to help you manage money …"

I felt like a complete failure as a father. The voice in my head was saying, *You're the biggest jerk father that has ever walked the Earth! How could you do this to your daughter?*

I don't consider myself an emotional person, but I must admit, that one got to me.

In the waiting room and during the ensuing days, I questioned everything I was doing as a parent and as a financial teacher. While I decided to forge ahead with the program, it took some time for that emotional toll to wear off.

Once my grief subsided, I came to the following conclusion: Lauren had a normal thought for any responsible individual — and it was preparing her for adulthood. Have you ever been injured and worried more about how much it would cost you once you got the medical bills than about the treatment itself?

We assured Lauren her medical expenses would be covered, and then I listed all of the other expenses we would continue to cover. I gave her a copy of that list.

It included:
- Medical and hospital
- Housing
- Food
- Transportation

You will have your own list.

By the way, it turned out Lauren's injury was major. Her ACL was intact, but it pulled away a piece of bone. She went through two surgeries and a whole lot of rehab.

REAL STORIES

Piano Lessons

Lauren took to the system well. She was not intimidated, and it made her money conscious almost immediately. She began supplementing her income by babysitting and working the concession stand at the local ballpark.

She also decided to realign her expenses into what *she* considered *priorities*. One of her expenses was piano lessons. One day, Lauren came to Denise and me and explained that she had taken lessons for almost seven years and was not going to continue. (Denise was not happy with this news!)

Lauren promised she would continue to play at home, but the cost for lessons was too high. I asked her if there was something else she wanted to spend the money on, and she replied, no, she was just going to *save* the extra money.

At the time, I immediately saw how the system was working. She was making an adult decision based on *what was important to her* — and this is exactly what we wanted! Lauren also showed us that she was a Saver. It was more rewarding for her to add to her savings than take the piano lessons. A Spender might make the same decision, but generally, there would be another use for the money already identified.

Although decisions like this may be a tough part of the experience for us as parents, our children are individuals, and their preferences will not always match ours. If she was taking the lessons just to please us, then her heart was not in it, so why continue?

I would advise that parents be united on the system and how it will be managed with the children before getting started. When presented with an unexpected decision, like the question of whether Lauren would continue piano lessons, we had the conversation privately and then came back to Lauren with our answer. In this case, we agreed to let Lauren stop taking piano lessons if she would continue to play at home.

* * * * * * * * * * * * * * * * * *

School Lunch

About three weeks after school started, Lauren came to me again, and this time she asked if she could pack her lunch rather than buy it at school and save the money. I agreed. I was so proud. Our 12-year-old daughter had just learned an important lesson that some of us don't learn for years. We stop at the local coffee shop for our mocha lattes, then follow it with expensive lunches at noon.

Then we wonder where our paychecks go!

Lauren was creating her own system to save money and plan for her future.

* * * * * * * * * * * * * * * * * *

The Math Error

The whole idea of managing money completely freaked out **Hayley**, our highly intelligent and emotional middle child. As much as we reassured her, she was certain she was going to make a fatal error.

As with most things in life, if you are sure you can or can't do something, you're generally right. Ten days after we opened Hayley's account, she came out of her room crying uncontrollably. Once I got her settled down, she told me her account was overdrawn.

"I'm sorry, Dad," she sniffled. "I don't know what I did wrong, but I have a negative balance in my checkbook."

I displayed more control and patience than I am usually capable of when she handed me her checkbook showing she was more than $100 overdrawn in 10 days! We gave her $300 to begin with, and she spent $400 in 10 days!

While I tried not to show it, I remember thinking: *This is basic math. Did you skip third grade?*

Instead, what I said was: "Let's see what went wrong. You've only written three checks. It looks like a math error."

A math error?

Hayley didn't make math errors. She was a straight-A student.

But I knew what had gone wrong. Just the idea of dealing with money has a huge impact on some people. It's much more than simply adding and subtracting numbers, it's *emotional*.

Therefore, numbers are added incorrectly or are put in the wrong columns because they rush through the painful process so it's over quickly. As a result, blood pressure skyrockets every time bills have to be paid or accounts balanced.

This actually describes a lot of adults! Some find it so painful that they put it off for as long as they can, making late payments and fees an unnecessary reality. The reason it's a painful process is there isn't a plan in place. Without a system to plan and track expenses, paying bills or balancing accounts becomes an activity that reveals a lack of money to cover necessary expenses. Once you have a simple plan and system in place, paying bills and balancing your accounts becomes a simple task.

In Hayley's case, it was indeed a math error! She and I were both relieved.

* * * * * * * * * * * * * * * * * *

From Whatever to Yes!

Our youngest, **Anna,** is four and a half years younger than Hayley and six years younger than Lauren. I am guessing that watching her sisters go through the First Habits system had an impact on her.

After we opened her account at the bank, I sat down with Anna to discuss her plan and received one of two responses throughout the entire process: "OK" and "I don't care."

I don't have many stories from Anna's time using the system. She rolled with anything, no extreme responses or actions.

A couple of years ago, when Anna was still in college but home for a break, I asked her, "Do you feel like the First Habits system has helped you at all?"

I honestly expected another, "I don't know."

But I received an enthusiastic "Yes!"

She told me how other girls in her sorority were having issues with money and how much easier it was for her because she had been doing it for years. They didn't have a plan, and many of them didn't even know how to balance their checking account. They would find out their account was overdrawn at the ATM and then have to call their parents for money. Until that conversation, I wasn't sure if the system had made any difference at all to Anna.

Practice Makes Perfect

Each child will act differently according to their Money Personality. You should go with them to deposit their first allowance check in their account. If they are excited, make sure they understand this is not a license to spend everything you give them on day one. If they are scared, reassure them you will help every step of the way and reinforce that making a mistake will not be fatal.

Be prepared for your child to work the program for their individual needs by either adding to their income or cutting expenses. This is exactly what you want them to do. It means they are beginning to make adult decisions and taking appropriate actions to change their situation.

SAVINGS ARE NON-NEGOTIABLE

Your child's savings account is an important safety net. Imagine your child bouncing three checks at a cost of $35 each because they made a mistake in recording a check or deposit. Yes, I know checks are obsolete, but many smaller organizations don't accept debit cards and don't allow Venmo or PayPal as an option. Now add a late fee for a payment that could not be made on time because of the unexpected cost of the bounced checks, and you can end up in a large hole quickly. With a savings account as backup, those mistakes are less costly.

Later in life, these problems get solved with credit cards in the form of a cash advance for a ridiculously high fee. Or worse yet, the absolute predatory business of "payday loans." These companies prey on those who can least afford it, with interest costs of 200% or more!

Savings is a safety net and an absolute necessity for financial success. There is only so much you can account for with a plan. As adults, we know surprises come in the form of medical bills, automobile expenses, vet bills, home repairs, funerals and on and on. This is why savings is a non-negotiable.

There is a right way and a wrong way to save. The "left-over" method is the wrong way. Trust me, I had to figure this out the hard way, too. As I noted earlier, the left-over method is simply paying your expenses from pay period to pay period and saving whatever is left over. It doesn't work for Spenders because we don't have anything left over. It doesn't work for Savers because they will deny themselves too much. This could work for the Whatevers if they had a disciplined habit of paying bills and were making more than their lifestyle required.

The better way to save — I'd argue, the right way — is based on planning your expenses and savings and systematically saving a portion of your income each pay period. Paying yourself first.

If I Had It To Do Over

If I had it to do over again, I would start the conversation with savings. I would explain to my child that we are going to set a plan based on $300 a month, and, after they pay themselves 10% (or $30), they have $270 to plan for monthly expenses. I would consciously try to develop the "Pay Yourself First" money script in their Money Mindset.

Next, I would build in mandatory charitable contributions in the budget. We would actually hand the girls money every Sunday to put in the offering at church. Why not make them plan and account for it? I added it to Lauren's plan for the example earlier in this chapter because I believe that charitable giving and savings should be the foundation for any system used to teach your children about money. Again, I think this is a great way to build a good habit. I would also allow our daughters to choose their own charity.

And, of course, I would have them track and manage everything in the Cabbage app.

Guiding Principles

Before I designed this system, I realized there were several key lessons that I wanted to instill in our daughters. I felt these guiding principles would help them deal with the difficult decisions they would ultimately face as adults and help them *stay true to themselves.*

You can agree or disagree with the following lessons, but the key is to have your own guiding principles for your children.

Here are my top three:

1. Possessions Do Not Equal Wealth

I remember one of our daughters telling me that her friends' parents were rich. When I asked why she thought that, she told me all about their new BMW.

I took this opportunity to explain that "stuff" does not equal *wealth* by explaining that they may very well be rich, but they also may spend every dollar they make on payments for those items.

I wanted our daughters to look past the big house and nice car (or modest home and older car) and *value each person by their character.*

2. Splurging Is OK, with Some Limits

Many of us, at some point in our lives, have justified a purchase based on the belief that we "deserved it." In many cases, it was a splurge we couldn't justify any other way.

If you want your child to be confident and successful about money management, talk to them about how often they "treat" themselves to splurges. There will be a big difference in their ability to create savings and control debt based on splurges that occur daily, weekly or monthly.

It's worth having a conversation about what you've found works and what doesn't for you. To control my Spender personality, I have created a "cooling off period." Based on the size of expense, I impose a 24-hour, one-week or one-month waiting period. For instance, If I'm working in the yard and decide I really need a new lawn mower, I have to wait a week to go buy it. Often, the immediate desire becomes something I can do without. If it doesn't, and I can afford it, I go ahead and buy it. I find myself applying the 24-hour cooling off period quite frequently. It helps me control impulse purchases. For example, it's not unusual for me to go to a hardware store or department store for a specific item and find something else that I "need." It might be a new grill accessory, a pair of shoes or even something in the checkout aisle. After that 24-hour cooling off period, I almost never go back the next day to make the purchase. This has been a lifesaver with Amazon!

3.   The Most Important Decision Is the Next One

Life comes with problems, but there *are* solutions. Imagine your child has spent unbudgeted money on some new shoes, and now they don't have enough to pay for essentials.

This is why I wanted to introduce this First Habits system to our daughters at a young age. The first step is working through the emotional "I screwed up" reaction to start considering options.

Here are four solutions for unplanned items:

By the way, this is where the patience and discipline come into play. Be disciplined enough to not bail your children out, and be patient with them as they work through the emotions and solve the problem.

1. Return the purchase as an immediate and complete solution. It's almost always the best option, and they may discover they don't miss the item after the fact. (This may be a good time to introduce a cooling off period.)
2. Help them find ways to cut other expenses to pay for the new item.
3. Support them in selling something they own to fund the purchase.
4. Suggest having them earn extra money to pay for the item.

Do not borrow the money to pay for the shoes. Not even from Mom and Dad. This introduces debt as a solution.

As with everything in life, problems tend to become larger and more expensive as we grow older. The problem changes from shoes, which can be returned, to a water pump on the car or a large medical bill.

When our children confessed to a mistake or problem, I told them that the most important decision was *the next one.* I wanted to shift the focus from their last decision — which they admitted was a bad one — to the next decision, which was the only one we could control.

Staying on Track

Once you've shown your child how to record their expenses and track the balance of their account with the Cabbage app or a spreadsheet, get them in the habit of tracking their expenses *daily.*

Explain how important it is to be diligent about the fact that the online balance is often higher than the actual balance because some purchases can take several days to clear the bank.

Having the bank send an alert to your phone (and your child's) is another way to stay on top of things. During the first month of the program, check in frequently to make sure your child is recording things correctly. Check the account balances and savings for upcoming expenses *before* giving them next month's allowance.

With online banking and very limited use of checks many of us never reconcile our bank statement to our account register — that's the little booklet that comes with your checks to record each check you write and keep a running balance. I would encourage you to have your child keep an account register and record any checks they write, withdrawals they make or debit card transactions and keep a running balance. It's a good lesson to understand that some checks and even some debit card transactions aren't reflected in your online bank balance immediately.

I have included a quick reconciliation spreadsheet here, or you can download a copy of a bank reconciliation form at the First Habits Win website, www.FirstHabitsWin.com.

Account Reconciliation Spreadsheet

Monthly Bank Reconciliation	
For the month of	June
Date of Statement	24-June
Ending Balance	$2,000
Listing of DEPOSITS in transit/ not appearing on statement	
Deposit Date	Amount
6/20/20	$20.00
	$0.00
	$0.00
	$0.00
Total outstanding deposits	**$20.00**
List of CHECKS outstanding/ not appearing on statement	
Check #	Amount
1234	$44.15
	$0.00
	$0.00
	$0.00
Total of outstanding checks	**$44.15**
Calculated Account Balance	**$1,975.85**

Planning Ahead

Planning is the hardest thing to manage because many of the items you are forecasting are variable costs rather than fixed costs. No matter how much effort you put into estimating these expenses, they will not be 100% accurate. Depending on the situation, consider letting your child work through their planning shortfalls by cutting out expenses in other areas. Even though you don't want to punish them harshly for making a mistake, you also don't want to bail them out, because if you do, they'll never learn.

Let them learn from mistakes so they make better decisions next time.

One great way to manage planned items that don't require a monthly payment is to set up additional online accounts and label them. This has worked for me personally and for one of our daughters in particular.

For example, if you have a $500 expense due in five months, label the account with the name of the expense and deposit $100 in it each month. Other options include the envelope system for saving at home. The envelope system gets its name because it uses physical envelopes to hold money for your spending categories (food, fuel, etc.). Once the money in the envelope is spent, that's it for the month.

The Cabbage app is based on the envelope system. In the app, you can separate multiple savings and expense items into individual electronic "accounts." You can also assign charges and deposits to your bank account to a specific expense item to track each separately.

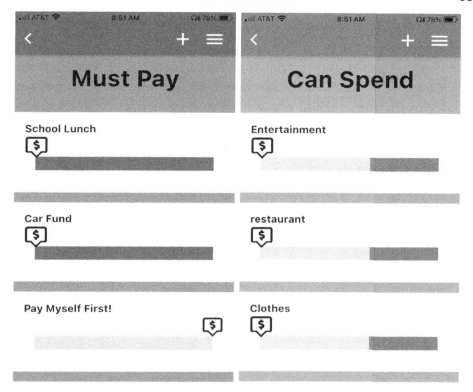

Each category — Expected Income, Other Income, Must Pay, Can Spend and Future Expenses — has a summary page that graphically represents where actual transactions are compared to the plan for the current month.

Staying Strong

You'll no doubt hear from many people who want to share their opinion about the system you're implementing with your children.

When friends and relatives want to bestow "advice," share how you are encouraging your child to learn *good money habits now, rather than later.* You may encounter resistance from others close to you, including grandparents, aunts, uncles, close friends and even your spouse if you are not both committed to the program.

You may hear comments like, "Little Billy isn't ready for this. Why are you in such a hurry for him to grow up?"

Those friends and relatives may jeopardize your system intentionally or unintentionally. It's fine for grandparents to give money to their grandchildren, as long as it's not with the intention of bailing them out or subsidizing their budget.

Explain to well-meaning relatives and friends what you are doing and ask them not to give your child money for these purposes. If your children come up short on their budget and can't pay for something they need or want, it's a learning opportunity for them and not a hero's opportunity for good ol' Aunt Betty.

SECTION FIVE

Navigating the Transitions

Formal education will make you a living; self-education will make you a fortune.

– Jim Rohn, entrepreneur and author

MIDDLE SCHOOL

Since the First Habits system is fiscally based on the concept of learning about money as a teenager and practically based on my experience teaching it to our three teenage daughters, I thought I'd share some behind-the-scenes stories that took place during their middle school years. I want to arm you with some insight into the potential pitfalls and opportunities you could face as your children use the system, so you can be better prepared.

Friendly Banker

As I created and implemented this system, one thing I never counted on was having our kind-hearted daughters become loan officers for their friends. I soon learned, for example, that when they would go out for pizza with friends, they would often be coaxed into treating one or more of them who didn't have money.

In some cases, they were paid back. I suspect that in the majority of cases, they were not. I explained to them that it was their decision if they wanted to buy for a friend.

I offered to be the bad guy — telling them they could blame me for the reason they couldn't loan money to friends. I also suggested that maybe they could treat their friends once in a while, but not to make a habit of it.

Prepare your children for this potential peer pressure.

One acquaintance of Lauren's stated that since her parents wouldn't give her money, Lauren should buy for her.

Wow.

* * * * * * * * * * * * * * * * * * *

You Can't Get Cool Jeans for $29!

Using the First Habits system came with several perks for our family, including the fact that it taught our daughters how to be price conscious from an early age.

When **Hayley** was in junior high, she was invited to a national youth leadership event in Boston. It was a great experience, and she made friends that she continues to keep in touch with today.

Several of the girls were from affluent families, and they were curious about Hayley's "small-town" life in Kansas.

One day, she met them for breakfast, and they complimented her jeans. They wanted to know the brand. Hayley laughed and told them she wasn't sure of the brand, but she got them at JCPenney for $29.

One replied skeptically, "But you can't get cool jeans for $29!"

"I don't own a pair of jeans that cost less than $100," another commented.

At that point, Hayley explained that she had to buy all of her own clothes and manage a plan for her expenses. The girls decided I was a mean dad and there was no way their parents would ever do that to them.

* * * * * * * * * * * * * * * * * * *

Kicked Out

When **Lauren** was 13, she went to the movies with a group of six friends. Fran, a mother of one of the girls, drove them to the theater and back to our house to spend the night.

We were surprised when Lauren and her friends came bounding through the door an hour earlier than expected. They made a beeline for the family room TV and all talked at once, laughing hysterically.

Fran, the chauffeur mom, was the last one through the door. She greeted Denise and me with an animated, "What have you done to your kid, and can you do the same to mine?"

She told us the reason the girls came home early was because they had been kicked out of the movie theater. A group of boys they knew sat in the row in front of them and kept turning around, talking to the girls and disturbing the audience.

When the usher came in with a flashlight, he told the boys *and* girls they would need to leave.

Once they were in the lobby, Lauren told the usher, "We were telling the boys to be quiet and they wouldn't shut up, so it's not our fault.

"If I can't see the movie, I want my money back!"

The usher disregarded the 13-year-old girl, so Lauren demanded to see the manager. In the end, she got her money refunded along with all of her girlfriends' ticket fees.

After Fran recounted the story, we spent the next hour explaining the First Habits system to her. Fran started the program with her daughter the very next week. She was the first to suggest that I should write a book and share this system with other parents. It's only taken me 17 years to heed her advice.

If I Had It To Do Over

Looking back to our daughters' middle school years, if I had it to do over, I would go over expenses with them at the end of each month to update the plan and do a comparison of actual expenses versus planned expenses. I did this for the first few months with each of the girls, but once they got comfortable with the system and weren't having any problems, I stopped doing the monthly reviews.

If you decide to include this step, don't use the time to shame them about what they spent their money on over the past 30 days. Instead use it as a proactive way to plan for future months and years, adding new items for new income sources and expenses. Your children — and you — will have a much better idea where your money is going.

Regular review is a foundational premise to all money management systems, and I'm sure it would have added a lot of value if I had continued it for our daughters.

HIGH SCHOOL

The high school years could represent a drastic change in spending for your teenager. Many students get part-time jobs, and this is also when you may consider purchasing a car for your young adult.

I would highly encourage you to consider allowing your high schooler to get a part-time job. I believe the responsibility of a job plus the satisfaction of earning without Mom and Dad's help is rewarding and empowering.

I'm not a fan, however, of forcing children younger than high school age to earn their own money. I didn't link my daughters' chores to their allowance. While it may be a good idea and work for some, I didn't want to tie their ability to pay for necessities to a chore. If they failed to do their chore, that would leave me with a situation where I would either have to cave and pay them for work not done or not pay them and jeopardize their ability to pay for school supplies and other necessities.

First Jobs

After working the concession stand at the local ballpark and babysitting, **Lauren** graduated to larger jobs. She worked retail, food service, health care and pretty much anything that was available. Love it or hate it, she would always show up and get the job done. Work was a source of pride for Lauren from an early age. It helped teach her responsibility.

* * * * * * * * * * * * * * * * * * *

Hayley's first job was at a local restaurant. She was a hostess and did the final "meal prep," or garnish on the plates, making sure they presented well.

She hated the job! After that, she worked at a retail clothing store and received a discount on clothes.

Although I didn't want Hayley to quit the restaurant job until she had something else lined up, I let her make her own decision. As it turned out, she was able to manage the lack of additional income until she found the retail job. In the end, I think it was a good learning experience.

It's never easy to take a step back in income, but Hayley learned from this experience at a young age, when the consequences were not so high.

* * * * * * * * * * * * * * * * * * *

Anna's first job was at a Greek restaurant and food market in a nearby college town. Like her sister, Anna also disliked working in the food service industry.

She later landed a job at a clothing retailer and took advantage of the employee discounts.

Tip: If you have fashion-conscious kids, encourage them to look for a job at their favorite clothing store. The discounts can definitely help with their clothing expenses, so long as they aren't tempted to spend their whole paycheck at the store.

Understanding Taxes

If and when your child takes on a job other than babysitting or mowing lawns for the neighbors, they will get exposed to the wonderful world of payroll tax deductions. This is a good time to explain the reason for taxes and what they provide.

I explained to our daughters that local taxes are used to pay for roads and bridges, schools, police and firefighters. At the federal level, I shared how our taxes are used for military, federal law enforcement and interstate highways, for example.

This simplistic explanation is easy for kids to understand and gives them some sense of what their taxes cover. To accurately plan for monthly expenses, they will need to understand how much will be withheld from their paychecks.

When our daughters each got their first check, I sat down and calculated the percentage being withheld for taxes, Medicare and Social Security. You may want to consider doing the same.

Although your child may not be required to file a tax return, it is good practice to go through the exercise with them. There are several apps that make filing a simple tax return a simple 10-minute process. Some allow you to simply take a photo of your 1099 and most everything is filled in for you. The apps are free, but there is a charge to electronically file your returns.

Here are a few popular options.

- https://turbotax.intuit.com
- www.freetaxusa.com
- www.taxslayer.com
- www.taxact.com
- www.hrblock.com

If your child is required to file a return, they will likely get a refund. This provides a good opportunity to talk to them about how to handle *unexpected income*. A good rule to follow is to save at least a portion of it.

For example, if your teenager gets a $400 tax refund, they will likely be inclined to spend it immediately — especially if they have a Spender money personality. You might suggest that they save 75% of it and spend the other 25%, leaving them with $100 to spend.

If I Had It To Do Over

When your children enter high school, life becomes more expensive. From cell phones, hair and makeup to cars, insurance and prom!

In retrospect, I didn't handle this as well as I could have. For the most part, we kept the girls' allowance flat and then helped them with additional expenses rather than incorporating those fully into the plan and increasing their allowance. For instance, when we added them to our cell phone plan, I just had the girls pay the additional line cost of $10 a month. With additional income from their part-time jobs, they were able to make this work, but I missed out on teaching them how much a cell phone plan really cost.

If I could go back, one thing I would change across the board is this covering of additional expenses for the girls. In hindsight, I could have created additional expense categories and increased the girls' allowances to account for these additional expenses, while leaving the responsibility for planning and paying for them to the girls.

I should have realized this time of life would be more expensive for them and continued the teaching opportunity. In the end, we paid for everything anyway. I just didn't make the most of the teaching opportunity.

For their cell phones, for example, I would increase their income enough to pay for a basic voice and data plan every month; if they wanted an unlimited plan or other features, they would have to figure out how to pay for that. I would also allow more for their clothes, makeup and school expenses. These additional expenses should be included in the plan and adjusted appropriately.

The only exception I would make to this general rule would be for things that Denise and I wanted for them but that they didn't necessarily want. This could be a suit for weddings and funerals, senior pictures or a class ring.

What Do *You* Deem Important?

If you find yourself in a situation where you cannot afford these increases, it's OK. This is not the thin line between success and failure as a parent.

Regardless of the situation, you can help your child through it and be there to support them. This may mean your child's part-time job provides the majority of their income, or it may mean sharing a car with Mom and Dad during high school.

Whatever your financial situation, the experience will mold your child's thought process as they continue to make their way into the world.

CREDIT CARDS

As I shared earlier, my financial problems began with a credit card offer I received in the mail after graduating from college. In all honesty, I was scared to death of getting a credit card when I first attended college, but by the time I was an upperclassman, it didn't seem like a big deal. Everyone had one!

Love them or hate them, credit cards are a fact of life for many. The problem is not with the credit card but rather with the lack of discipline when using them.

The Credit CARD Act of 2009 put the brakes on credit card use by college students. Among other provisions, it bans credit card approvals for anyone *under* age 21 unless they have an adult co-signer or can prove they have sufficient income to pay the bills.[6]

More college students in 2019 had debit cards (85%) than credit cards (57%), according to the "Majoring in Money" survey by student loan provider Sallie Mae.[7] The top reasons students cited for not having a credit card were wanting to avoid debt (46%) and not feeling like they needed one (38%).

There are promising signs in this survey showing that students who have credit cards tend to pay them off responsibly. Nearly two-thirds (60%) paid their card balance in full each month. Just 11% paid only the minimum amount due each month.

According to Sallie Mae's 2020 report "How America Pays for College," on average, 21% of college costs are paid by borrowing (either by the student or the parent). Most of that comprises student loans, but 7% of students used credit cards to help fund college costs, while 2% of students' parents did the same.[8]

Are Credit Cards a Good Idea?

When our daughters turned 16, I got a credit card for each of them by opening a new account with our existing credit card company. Denise and I opened a joint account and added the girls as additional cardholders. The girls had their own card with their name on it, and I insisted on the account having a $500 limit.

I chose to get a credit card for the girls for two reasons.

First, I wanted them to have this experience early in life to limit the size of mistakes they might make. Second, I wanted them to have it for convenience and learn how to work it into their plan after having four years of experience with the First Habits system.

Before turning the card over, I explained to the girls how borrowing money from the credit card company is actually *a loan*. Then I illustrated how interest works by showing them how a $500 charge on their card paid with $20 monthly payments (roughly what the card company will require as a minimum payment) and 12% annual interest, would take over two years (28 months) to pay off.

Credit Card Interest

Balance: $500 | Interest Rate: 12% | Minimum Payment: $20

Month	Balance	Interest	Payments	Month	Balance	Interest	Payments
0	$500.00	$5.00	($20.00)	15	$258.55	$2.59	($20.00)
1	$485.00	$4.85	($20.00)	16	$241.13	$2.41	($20.00)
2	$469.85	$4.70	($20.00)	17	$223.54	$2.24	($20.00)
3	$454.55	$4.55	($20.00)	18	$205.78	$2.06	($20.00)
4	$439.09	$4.39	($20.00)	19	$187.84	$1.88	($20.00)
5	$423.48	$4.23	($20.00)	20	$169.71	$1.70	($20.00)
6	$407.72	$4.08	($20.00)	21	$151.41	$1.51	($20.00)
7	$391.80	$3.92	($20.00)	22	$132.93	$1.33	($20.00)
8	$375.71	$3.76	($20.00)	23	$114.26	$1.14	($20.00)
9	$359.47	$3.59	($20.00)	24	$95.40	$0.95	($20.00)
10	$343.07	$3.43	($20.00)	25	$76.35	$0.76	($20.00)
11	$326.50	$3.26	($20.00)	26	$57.12	$0.57	($20.00)
12	$309.76	$3.10	($20.00)	27	$37.69	$0.38	($20.00)
13	$292.86	$2.93	($20.00)	28	$18.06	$0.18	($18.24)
14	$275.79	$2.76	($20.00)	Total Interest		$78.24	
				Total Payments		($578.24)	

This table illustrates how making the minimum payment on a $500 purchase will cost $78.24 in interest AND will take over two years to pay off. This assumes no additional purchases during those two years.

Both Lauren and Hayley were initially scared of the idea of having a credit card. Anna simply refused to even get one.

I told them they would need to figure out how to use the card. Their choices were to use it for convenience and pay it off every month or to use it for emergencies only. It was up to them.

Over time, they started to use the card to purchase fuel, dinner out, clothes, shoes and anything else you can imagine.

TIP: Be aware that when you set up your child's credit card this way, the credit experience will be reported under your name. I received notifications through the credit card company if payments weren't made on time.

Expect your child to make mistakes. They will charge too much, or struggle to make the minimum payment or miss paying on time. Remember, we want them to make small mistakes in the beginning. The only way to make an impact with this lesson is to let them feel the pain and anxiety associated with making poor decisions in the short-term in order to help them make better decisions in the long-term.

The One-Time Bailout

Lauren and **Hayley** each maxed out their credit cards when they were in college. They both paid on time, but with minimum payments.

They had each been in this situation for over a year when we decided to make a Christmas gift of paying off the cards for them, reinforcing that this would be *their last bailout*. I asked them to think about what it would feel like to be $5,000 in debt. Or $50,000 in debt.

I could tell by the look in their eyes they were taking it seriously.

I know I said previously that bailing them out was a bad idea, but between the ages of 12 and 16, Lauren and Hayley were open to the idea of being my test subjects to try the system so we could prove if it helped them manage money later in life.

As a result, in middle school they had small infractions, and in high school they used their credit cards with no problems. However, I made an error in keeping their allowance flat when they started college. Even though they had part-time jobs, their expenses for books, food, etc., were more than we had anticipated.

I'm sure most parents of college-age children can relate to this uptick in spending. (This was a learning curve for us as well as them.)

I was sure to reiterate that Santa said, "Merry Christmas this *one* time!"

I told them, "Now you are living on a very limited budget, but soon you will graduate and have a job with more income than you've ever had before. But you will also have more *expenses*. If you choose to spend beyond your income, you will end up in the same position, but the dollar amount will be even higher and harder to rectify.

"There are people who make a million dollars a year and are strapped making credit card payments. You have to make a choice to be disciplined and live within your means.

"I knew a highly successful, 70-year-old executive who worked night and day to pay a $12 million mortgage. He was not living within his means either. Things can get away from you quickly if you're not careful and then you're stuck in a no-win situation."

I also shared how I made the same mistake when they were young. And I shared my friend Joe's story to illustrate that regardless of your income you have to manage your money wisely.

Everything is relative.

Not Whatever, No

Anna absolutely refused to get a credit card. I think watching her sisters struggle with theirs in college scared her. As a Whatever, Anna decided the best way to deal with it was to just not deal with it. She was very firm when she told me she did not need or want a credit card.

"Just use it for gas," I said.

"Why? I have my debit card," she replied.

"Just keep it for emergencies," I said.

"What emergency?" she countered.

"You never know, Anna," I warned.

"DAD, I don't want a credit card!" she retorted with tears in her eyes.

That was it, debate over. Anna didn't get a credit card.

She made it all the way through college and just recently got a credit card with her husband. He's a Saver. They are both extremely responsible, and I don't have any concerns.

The First Car

For a teenager, a car represents independence and freedom. For us parents, it represents a new level of worry and makes sleep very hard to achieve until they return home!

We did not have a plan when it came to getting a car for **Lauren**. When she asked if we would help her buy a car, I thought it over and decided we would pay half but we would have final approval. Safety and reliability were priorities.

I also agreed to increase her income for gas but said that we would pay for taxes, insurance and maintenance. Looking back, I'd add those expenses to the girls' plan to cover the additional costs associated with car ownership. Then our daughters would have had a better understanding of the cost for non-routine expenses. This was another "if I had it to do over again" moment.

After all, isn't paying for your first car — and the expenses associated with it — a huge lesson in money management?

Our paying the taxes, insurance and maintenance was also contingent on their having no traffic tickets or wrecks.

About a week after we first talked to Lauren about buying a car, she approached us again. She'd found a *new* Chevy Cobalt.

"Really?" I asked. "Do you realize that's a $12,000 car? Do you have $6,000?"

"Most of it," she answered.

"Where did you get $6,000?!!" I asked.

"I've saved all of my babysitting money, birthday money, concession stand money. It's in my piggy bank and savings account," she explained.

"Bring your bank and show me," I told her.

As she went to retrieve her bank, I looked at Denise and said, "$6,000! I didn't plan on $6,000 being half!"

Lauren returned a few minutes later and began pulling out rolls of bills tightly bound with rubber bands. The rolls added up to $100 each in ones, fives, tens and twenties. She counted them out and then showed us her savings book balance.

I was in shock.

The following week, Lauren bought a brand new car. This was an enormous source of pride and a major accomplishment for her. There's definitely something to be said for pride of ownership.

You might be thinking, wait a minute, Lauren is a Saver. They don't like to spend money, right? Even Savers have things that they value more than their fat savings account — or wads of cash in a piggy bank in Lauren's case. I would bet that Lauren spent a considerable amount of time weighing the benefits of having her own car versus having all of that savings.

Two years later, it was **Hayley's** turn. By this time, Hayley had learned to manage her money and was doing well. However, she was still a Spender.

On top of that, she had requirements that needed to be met for her 6 feet of height and seriously long legs. She decided an SUV was the only option. It was hard to find one in her price range, but she had saved nearly $3,000 and we were proud of her accomplishment.

Spenders tend to fall in love with their first option, but we did our homework and looked at several makes and models until we found a Jeep Liberty that fit her well.

I blame myself for giving zero consideration to fuel efficiency and how much she would need to spend when compared to a more economical car.

Last but not least was **Anna**. Never too high, never too low and always even-keeled, Anna had less to spend than her sisters. With her Whatever personality, she was more patient than Hayley but not a planner like Lauren.

After looking at several cars, she found a used Toyota Corolla. We purchased the car, and she drove it to her boyfriend's house, pulled into his driveway and right into the back of his car.

Suddenly, Anna was no longer even-keeled. Her reaction at the time was more suited to vehicular homicide than a fender-bender. Fixing the front bumper was up to her. The damage was minor, so Anna decided not to spend the money to have it fixed. She drove more carefully after that.

There will be lessons with cars; some are too devastating to learn the hard way. I believe that having your child pay for a large portion of their first car will influence how well they take care of it. Buying a car is also a true sense of accomplishment for them, creating confidence and pride at a time when they need that reinforcement.

If I Had It To Do Over

In hindsight, I would add a savings plan for a car to each of the girls' overall plans starting at the age of 12. It would be another lesson in patience and discipline that would pay off for them at 16 or 17. It would also be a nice way for us to save and be better prepared for the cost of having an older teenager.

The other thing I would do is consider more than just safety and reliability. Fuel efficiency and the cost of insurance and maintenance can be a significant expense with a vehicle. This is a great opportunity to explain the total cost of ownership to your teenager.

Finally, I would make the expense of maintenance and insurance the child's responsibility and increase their allowance to cover it.

Tip: I know cars come not just with additional financial worries. Safety is always top of mind. There are a number of apps hitting the market that allow you to track your child's location via GPS. You can even lock their phones while the car is moving if you're worried about texting when driving. Here are some to check out; they are all available for both Apple and Android users.

- TrueMotion Family Safe Driving app
- AT&T Drive Mode app
- Life360, www.life360.com
- MamaBear app

Auto Loans

Most people realize cars are depreciating assets, losing value over time — even as you drive them off the lot! Borrowing money for a depreciating asset, something that loses value over time, can be dangerous. I won't go as far as personal finance author Dave Ramsey and tell you to take the bus until you can pay cash for a car, but you do need to be smart about borrowing.

Think of a car loan as a race. You are trying to pay off the loan faster than the car depreciates, or you will owe more on the car than it's worth, becoming "upside-down" or "underwater" in the car.

In this case, if the car is involved in a wreck or damaged in any way, you could end up with no car while owing the bank money after the insurance company pays the claim. The insurance will only pay for the market value of the car.

To avoid this situation, you need to do two things:

1. Do your homework
2. Know what you can afford

1) **Do your homework.** Know what the market price is for the car you want and know how quickly it will depreciate. Some cars maintain their value better than others, so this will be specific to the car you are looking to purchase. There are several websites that offer free depreciation calculators for cars.

Here is an example from www.goodcalculators.com.

I plugged in a 2-year-old car with a $30,000 sale price and a five-year loan. The depreciation schedule shows the value of the car at the end of each year.

Car Depreciation			
Vehicle Age	Depreciation Rate	Value Lost	Car Value
1	15.6%	$4,680.00	$25,320.00
2	15.6%	$8,629.92	$21,370.08
3	15.6%	$11,963.65	$18,036.35
4	15.6%	$14,777.32	$15,222.68
5	15.6%	$17,152.06	$12,847.94
Average annual value lost		$11,440.59	

Make sure that your loan balance is always lower than "your car's value" on the depreciation schedule.

2) **Know what you can afford.** Work out a plan to know what you can truly afford. You will need to pay sales tax, property tax, registration fees and insurance. Lastly, you will need to pay for normal maintenance and repairs.

Let's consider a purchase of a new car with a price of $31,000. Based on some quick research, this is roughly the average price for a new car in 2020. Sales tax on the purchase (assume 7% sales tax rate) will be $2,170.

The average new car loses 9% of its value the minute you drive it off the lot and 19% by the end of the first year. To avoid being upside-down in your loan the minute you drive off the lot, you will want to put at least 9% down on the loan, or $2,790.

If you live in a state that charges property tax, you will need to pay for that when you register the vehicle. Let's assume the property tax is 2%, or $620.

You will also need to pay for the first month's insurance. Let's assume $75 for full coverage, which you will be required to have for your loan. Add it all up, and you will need a minimum of $5,655 to purchase a new $31,000 car.

Car price: $31,000

- $2,170 – Sales tax (7%)
- $2,790 – Initial lost value (9%)
- $620 – Property tax (2%)
- $75 – Insurance (1 month)

Total: $5,655

You will also need to have enough money in your plan to continue to pay for the ongoing insurance, property taxes (due annually) and normal maintenance for the car. There are numerous websites that will estimate maintenance for the make and model you're considering. Edmunds offers a True Cost to Own˙ calculator to estimate those additional costs at www.edmunds.com. (For the purposes of our next discussion, let's say you'll need $160 a month for insurance, taxes and maintenance.)

Can't Afford a New Car?

After doing your homework, you decide you can't afford a new, $31,000 car. You have $4,000 saved and $550 available in your monthly plan. You know that the car you want will lose 19% of its value in the first year, so if it's $31,000 new, it should be worth about $25,000 when it's a year old. This lower price/value will also lower your taxes and insurance.

You decide to buy the same vehicle, just one model year older. Great decision! Now it's time to visit the dealership.

Let me walk you through the conversation as you meet the salesperson and describe what you're looking for.

Salesperson: "Great, do you have a trade-in or down payment?"

You: "I have $4,000, but most of that will go for taxes and insurance."

Salesperson: "What kind of payment are you looking for?"

You: "I have $550 in my plan, but I need $160 of that for maintenance, taxes and insurance."

Salesperson: "Have you considered buying new?"

You: "I wanted to, but I can't afford it."

Salesperson: "But if I could get you to the payment you planned, would you consider buying new?"

You: "Sure, I guess."

The salesperson leaves and returns with a printout: "I just spoke to my general manager, and I think we can put you in a new car today."

$0 Down
72 Months = $527.11
84 Months = $476.00

Salesperson (smiling from ear to ear): "What do you think?"

You: "I can't go that high on the payment and cover my taxes, insurance and maintenance."

Salesperson: "I have added the sales tax to the loan, so that's taken care of. You won't have any maintenance for the first couple of years; this is a brand-new car! How much is your insurance?"

You: "About $75 a month, but I also have to pay property tax."

Salesperson: "You still have your $4,000 for property tax since I financed your sales tax. That leaves you with $476 + $75 for insurance, so you're at $550. Let's go find your new car!"

You: "I don't know, seven years (84 months) seems like a long car loan."

Salesperson: "Don't worry, you will probably trade it in three years from now. Are we good?"

If you agree to this, let me show you exactly what you have agreed to in the Car Loan Calculator Chart.

Car Equity			
	Loan Balance	Car Value	Equity in the Car
Day 1	$33,790	$28,210	-$5,580
Year 1	$29,995	$25,110	-$4,885
Year 2	$25,656	$19,840	-$5,816
Year 3	$21,100	$15,190	-$5,910
Year 4	$16,315	$12,090	-$4,225
Year 5	$11,291	$9,300	-$1,991
Year 6	$6,015	$7,096	$1,081
Year 7	$474	$4,393	$4,393

See in this chart, in the far right column, how you don't have positive equity in the car until year six? Up until then, you owe more on the car than it is worth. *This* is why you don't want to allow a car dealer to talk you into "a payment you can afford." All they are doing is *extending the loan further* to lower the monthly payment, and you will be *upside-down* in the loan as soon as you drive it off the lot.

I have been car shopping with all of our daughters, and I can tell you from experience that car salespeople are very good at getting people in bad loans. The preceding illustration was a *true experience* we recently had.

How Can You Guard Against This?

The first question the car salesperson asked was, "How much do you want your payment to be?"

To avoid this, get preapproved by your bank before you visit the car lot, then answer, "I already have my financing in place."

Why should you do this?

Because the salesperson's next question will be, "What if I could get you better financing?"

What they don't tell you is that *better* usually means *a longer loan* with lower monthly payments. **This is better for them, not you!** They will sell you a higher-priced car and let you deal with the upside-down problems down the road.

My answer is always: "I'm not interested in your financing. I just want to buy the car from you. Can we do that?"

Go into the dealership knowing what car you want and how much you will pay. There are tons of ways to shop and compare online. Or use a car buying service to know what you should pay for the car. USAA and Costco both include car buying services in their membership, for example. Another great resource is Kelly Blue Book, www.kbb.com.

Time for an Upgrade

After graduating from college and landing a good job, **Hayley** decided it was time to upgrade from Larry. (Larry was the name she gave her Jeep Liberty that she drove through high school and college.)

We found the car she wanted to buy, but it was $2,000 more than she had planned.

The salesperson did some math and came back with a $250 reduction in the price and a printout of what her payments would be at five, six and seven years.

I reiterated that the financing was taken care of and the only thing they had done was extend the loan.

His answer, "You know you won't keep the car more than three years, so it really doesn't matter."

I countered, "It does matter! She will pay more in interest and less in principal and be *upside-down* in the car!"

He replied, "At this rate the interest is very small, so it just doesn't make that much difference."

At that point, I said, "I can explain the math to you, but I don't think it will help," and we left the dealership.

Most people don't understand the consequences of extending their loan and buying more car than they can afford. They actually think the salesperson is helping them.

Educate yourself and look out for your own best interests. Hayley and I ended up finding the *exact same car* at another dealer — same color, same features, and it was actually cleaner. It was $2,000 less and had fewer miles and the remaining factory warranty.

COLLEGE

I'd suggest a couple of things to help your child make the transition into adulthood before attending college. When your son or daughter reaches age 18, consider converting all their bank accounts and credit cards to their name. Start by removing your name from their checking and savings accounts.

Then, if your son or daughter has a car titled in your name, you need to officially transfer ownership.

Finally, close any credit cards you have opened with your child and have them reopen their own accounts. You will need to guarantee or co-sign the account with them if they are under 21, but the general credit experience will be reported only in their name.

By doing these things, you are helping your child build their own credit and payment history. You will also limit your liability in the case of an accident or lawsuit.

We did not stop helping our daughters when they turned 18, and you can make these moves regardless of whether you intend to continue financially supporting your child.

We covered the cost of their college tuition and housing and continued providing the same monthly allowance they got in high school for other expenses. This, of course, did not cover all of their needs. They each worked part time while in school, and all three of our daughters were able to find paying jobs in their field.

I am a huge proponent of a college education. It creates access to opportunity not available without a college degree, but more importantly, it provides a basic network of friends with specific skills.

Have you noticed how many executives in the same company graduated from the same college? We all prefer to work with people we know and trust.

Over the years, I've had one key requirement before agreeing to pay for college for my daughters: they had to have a true passion for their field of study and a desire to pursue a career.

College Financing Options

When considering how to pay for college, apply the same basic principles that I have highlighted throughout this book: Know what you want and create a plan to get there.

In this case, the plan will include the entry-level job salary that will help them repay any student loans. I would suggest you work with your child to help with these decisions.

You should both educate yourselves on student loans, financial aid, scholarships, the job market in their chosen field, placement assistance from the college and many other things. There are a number of resources that will be made available to you once your child reaches their junior or senior year in high school.

Congratulations! You Made It!

At this point, the First Habits system teaching is complete. There will still be times when you can provide advice and support, but the formal training is over. I've developed an easy way to help your college kid remember how to manage their finances during their college years (and beyond): the acronym **MONEY**.

Make sure to pay yourself first.

Only use a credit card if you pay the total balance each month.

Never compare yourself to others.

Everyone makes mistakes; learn from them.

Your most important decision is the next one.

SECTION SIX

Proven Results

Good habits formed at youth make all the difference.

– Aristotle, Greek philosopher

WHERE ARE THEY NOW?

The habits our daughters formed as a result of this training will benefit them the rest of their lives — things like planning, balancing their accounts and saving for future expenses. But I think the bigger value is the lessons learned along the way. Understanding credit card debt or bouncing a check and the impact that can have. Or having savings in the bank when something unexpected comes up.

I couldn't have developed the First Habits system or written this book without the lessons I learned right alongside our daughters and with Denise's assistance. We are very proud of all three of them.

I thought it would be helpful for our daughters to share their perspectives after going through the First Habits system. I had a colleague interview each of them for this section of the book.

* * * * * * * * * * * * * * * * * *

Lauren is still a Saver. She is married, in her late twenties and works as a Recovery Coach Case Manager, helping people with behavioral health and substance abuse issues.

After getting her CNA (Certified Nursing Assistant) license and working in a nursing home, she decided to change direction from nursing and pursued a degree in psychology. She wanted to help people *before* they were sick rather than take care of them after a lifetime of poor choices.

Still living in Kansas, she gave us a peek into how the system worked for her.

"I think Dad's system was a good thing for our family. The day I turned 12, Dad let me skip school and we went to the bank together. It was like a rite of passage for each of us. He made it a fun day.

"Later, he taught me how to balance the checkbook. I remember being so excited to receive my first ATM card.

"The First Habits system was unusual to other people," Lauren said, "but it was normal in our family. My friends would ask why I had to pay for everything from movies to a prom dress. I was the only kid with a checkbook or an ATM card.

"I told friends that Dad was teaching me how to manage money. As a teen, I learned early that if I spent too much one month, I had to cut back the next month. I didn't like that, so I learned some self-control to give myself a cushion.

"I was concerned that people would think I was the rich kid," she confessed. "But the program helped tremendously. By the time I got to college, I had a job, started making my own money and opened a new checking account without Dad as a co-signer."

"I'm a natural-born Saver because it freaks me out to think about not having enough money. I'm still guilty of wearing clothes past their prime," Lauren laughed.

"I don't like to splurge even though my husband says it's OK. He's a Spender and he's more of a risk-taker. He even bought a house on his own when he was 27. Those kind of purchases scare me," she admitted.

"But he puts money away every month for our retirement. Lately, I've been rewarding myself by planning little trips with friends, including one this weekend.

"I'm always looking for good deals and have an everything credit card that I put all of my normal expenses on and then pay it off every month. I use the points I accumulate from those everyday purchases to pay for flights.

"Overall, Dad's program was helpful," Lauren concluded. "There weren't any negatives. It taught me the value of money, because as a teen, you don't understand how much things cost. Today, I'm not in financial debt, and I credit him for that.

"Doing the program together actually brought my Dad and I closer. (He also coached my softball team!) I think I grew up *lucky*. Working in the behavioral health field has been an eye-opener for me."

* * * * * * * * * * * * * * * * *

Hayley is still a Spender, like her dad. In college, she got a job at a lab on campus and was able to leverage that practical experience to land her first job with a large animal science company when she graduated. She's in her late twenties, living in Kansas and is an associate scientist at a pharmaceutical lab.

"Initially, I freaked out over the idea of having Mom and Dad's money to spend. I worried that they would be disappointed. But Dad told me not to be afraid to ask for help.

"He said, 'You're going to make mistakes. Everybody does.'

"He knows I stress over things. Because I was more intimidated, Dad had to spend more time with me. I was embarrassed to tell him that I screwed up in two short weeks. But it was a checkbook error, not a bank error. Crisis averted!"

She added: "Then Lauren and I both messed up with our credit cards in college. We were supposed to pay the balance off every month, and we got behind on our payments. Dad warned us not to just pay the minimum. I thought I could handle it, but it got away from me quickly!

"With most kids, their parents are already paying for school lunches, etc., but I was responsible for planning everything. My friends thought it was cool because I had my own money to buy things, but I soon learned that — because of this system — I was more financially independent than my friends.

"I still don't think I'm *the best* at managing money, so I have built-in safeguards like having bills paid automatically each month from my checking account. Regarding my savings, I set my online dashboard so I can't see it. Out of sight, out of mind.

"I have a credit card, and I don't let it get out of hand. But when it comes to purchases, I'll admit, I don't like to tell myself no. I learned a lot of this earlier than most, and I didn't have to stress in college when I was juggling classes, etc. It was helpful overall."

* * * * * * * * * * * * * * * * *

Anna is still a Whatever. Now in her early twenties, she got her degree in Early Childhood Development. She is recently married and also lives in Kansas and is a lead teacher in an early childhood education center.

"By the time it was my turn, I understood the basic concept of the First Habits system," she says. "Over the years, I'd watched my sisters plan for their money, and I admit, I was a little nervous because I didn't understand checking accounts. It took me a while to figure those out.

"I was always afraid I'd overdraw my account, and in middle school I did some damage two or three times before I got the hang of it. I went to Dad to confess. He reacted better than I expected. I learned to make sure I had that cushion. At that time, we had smaller repercussions.

"These mistakes happened before online banking was popular, so if I screwed it up, I'd have to race down to the bank to fix it. I wasn't good at math, and I didn't pay attention to it like I should have.

"When I went out with friends, they would have a set amount of money, like a $20 bill. Or they could only go out when they earned their allowance. I got to choose how to spend my money and always knew how much I had.

"As an adult, I'm able to look back and say I made those mistakes at 13 rather than 20 because I saw my friends go through some major money problems! Most didn't start managing a plan until they were 18 and went to college. In college I got really close to having no money at all, but it never happened.

"Today I realize rent and utility bills are a much bigger deal! So, I've become more of a Saver.

"I plan to teach my children this system."

Conclusion

I've felt compelled to write this book and share this system because it has provided great results for our family. To give children a strong foundation for financial success we, as parents, need to help them build keystone habits and let them learn by experience early in life, as we do with so many other things.

As you've seen, we are essentially born with a basic Money Personality. Even being raised in the same environment and doing the same program, all three of our daughters managed their money differently.

To this day, they still do, dependent on their personalities — and I am so proud of the young ladies they have become. Our daughters truly are the love of my life and without a doubt the greatest blessing my wife and I have received.

I want to specifically thank them for dealing with so many unknowns at such a young age. I know they were alone among their friends while dealing with the system, and I'm sure it presented challenges at times.

Still A Work In Progress

Over time, I've realized that my success with managing money has come through finding ways to *self-manage* my Spender personality traits. It now makes sense to me that no matter how well my parents modeled disciplined savings and living within their means, these behaviors did not come easily because they did not align with my core personality.

I also believe what we taught our daughters has been of great value to them and will be throughout their lives, regardless of their unique personalities. However, I can also see there are several things I could have done to further help them, which is why I've included the "If I Had It To Do Over" sections throughout the book.

I hope you will benefit from using this system with your own children. I'd love to hear your experiences. Email me at:
Mike.Miller@FirstHabitsWin.com.

How Can I Help You?

Now that our daughters are young adults and I've seen the success of this system, my desire has expanded once again. I see young couples beginning their married lives and starting families. I know they are dealing with the financial stresses of getting started.

From struggling with buying a first home to dealing with the cost of childcare, they want to do everything they can to help their young children.

At the same time, I also know affluent families that need a financial education and tips for self-discipline.

My intent is to continue to expand the resources on www.FirstHabitsWin.com. There you'll find links to a variety of resources, including sites to help with calculating the total cost of a car, calculating how fast a car will depreciate, preparing tax returns and many other practical topics. Also available on the First Habits Win website are the planning templates I used with our daughters.

About the Author

Mike Miller is an executive leader in the financial services industry and the creator of the First Habits system and author of "First Habits Win."

Mike has a bachelor's degree in finance from Kansas State University. He has served on the Insured Retirement Institute's Senior Steering Committee for Operations and Technology, and he is an advisory board member for the Kansas State University Professional Financial Planning Program, a top five program in the United States.

After creating the First Habits system for his daughters and seeing the benefits, Mike has become passionate about helping parents provide the education, training and real-world experience to set their children on a path to a positive Money Mindset and financial success.

With "First Habits Win" and the First Habits system, Mike aims to improve the financial lives of a generation by giving parents the tools and resources to provide the education their children will rely on for the rest of their lives.

Acknowledgments

I would like to express my sincere thanks to each of our daughters, Lauren, Hayley and Anna. I cannot adequately express my love for each of you. I truly hope that what we have taught you brings great benefit to your lives. Thank you for agreeing to be my case studies in this book.

Next, I want to thank my partner and best friend in life, my wife, Denise. Thank you for trusting and going along with me when the immediate results were not always easy and the long-term benefits were not guaranteed. And thank you for helping the girls with this system and being a resource for them when I wasn't available or they didn't want to come to me directly. I love you.

To my parents, who played a key role in each of the girls' lives, thank you for supporting us and always being there for the girls. The level of respect and admiration the girls have for you helped them make good decisions and will continue to guide them in their adult lives. I would also like to thank you for providing me with a stellar example of work ethic, temperance and the value of family. I love you both.

Resources

The Cabbage app is available in the App Store and Google Play. Find out more from www.FirstHabitsWin.com

"Wired For Wealth," by Brad Klontz, Psy.D., Ted Klontz, Ph.D., and Rick Kahler, CFP®

Tax software

- https://turbotax.intuit.com/
- www.freetaxusa.com
- www.taxslayer.com
- www.taxact.com
- www.hrblock.com

Car buying calculators and comparison

- Kelly Blue Book, www.kbb.com
- www.goodcalculators.com
- www.edmunds.com

Safe driving apps

- TrueMotion Family Safe Driving app
- AT&T Drive Mode app
- Life360, www.life360.com
- MamaBear app

Endnotes

[1] Thrive Global. February 2020. "Thriving Wallet." https://content.thriveglobal.com/wp-content/uploads/2020/02/Thriving-Wallet-Research-Insights-Report.pdf. Accessed Aug. 6, 2020.

[2] Ibid.

[3] Mark Lino. USDA.gov. Feb. 18, 2020. "The Cost of Raising a Child." https://www.usda.gov/media/blog/2017/01/13/cost-raising-child. Accessed Aug. 6, 2020.

[4] Suzanne Kearns. Money Crashers. "The Psychology of Money – How Saving and Spending Habits are Programmed in your Brain." https://www.moneycrashers.com/psychology-of-money-saving-spending-habits/. Accessed Aug. 6, 2020.

5 Catherine Byerly. Annuity.org. Sept. 16, 2020. "Inside the Brains of a Saver and a Spender." https://www.annuity.org/2015/09/21/how-savers-and-spenders-think/. Accessed Sept. 30, 2020.

[6] FTC.gov. May 22, 2009. Credit Card Accountability Responsibility and Disclosure Act of 2009. https://www.ftc.gov/sites/default/files/documents/statutes/credit-card-accountability-responsibility-and-disclosure-act-2009-credit-card-act/credit-card-pub-l-111-24_0.pdf. Accessed Aug. 6, 2020.

[7] Sallie Mae. 2019. "Majoring in Money: How college students and other young adults manage their finances." https://www.salliemae.com/assets/about/who_we_are/Majoring-In-Money-Report-2019.pdf. Accessed Aug. 6, 2020.

[8] Sallie Mae and Ipsos. 2020. "How America Pays for College." https://www.salliemae.com/about/leading-research/how-america-pays-for-college/. Accessed Aug. 6, 2020.

Made in the USA
Monee, IL
06 March 2022